ENDORSEMENTS

"In our lives there [barcode: T0163684] fought. This book takes us from of Afghanistan to Andrew's unrelenting battle to be whole again--for himself, his family, and so he could go on to help others suffering from TBIs on a major scale. It's a raw reminder that even in a brain injured state, the mind can clearly triumph."

– Joe Rogan
Comedian, UFC commentator,
Host of The Joe Rogan Experience Podcast

"Andrew Marr is a war hero and Special Forces veteran who was knocked unconscious eliminating a weapons cache in Afghanistan less then 50 meters away from him and his team while pinned down from effective enemy fire. This event and several more led to numerous documented disabilities including Traumatic Brain Injury and Post-Traumatic Stress. Returning home, he found himself on 13 medications including those for depression, insomnia, and anxiety. Andrew knew he was at a crossroads. This was the beginning of Andrew's own healing. He quit tobacco, stopped drinking, came off all medication, and embraced an emotional healing that began by identifying his own personal purpose which was to serve others. He embraced a physiological approach to inflammation and neurochemical replacement rather than a pharmacological one. He made a choice that brought him into the light. All major change, he says, "occurs from inspiration or desperation." For Andrew, it was both."

– Marc Siegel MD

Professor of Medicine and Medical Director of Doctor Radio on SiriusXM

NYU Langone Medical Center

Fox News Medical Correspondent

Author of *The Inner Pulse; Unlocking the Secret Code of Sickness and Health*

"Inspirational with optimism and ownership of one's direction in life. Andrew Marr drew upon his pain to feed his philosophy and learned to heal himself. He sums up his thoughts with real life experiences which he shares with the reader. You will find yourself returning to Chapter 10, repeatedly, to maintain a life of direction and therefore quality."

– Mark L. Gordon, MD.

Medical Director, Millennium Health Centers, Inc.

Millennium-WAF TBI Project

CBS Studios

The Clinical Application of Interventional Endocrinology (2007)

Traumatic Brain Injury: A Clinical Approach to Diagnosis and Treatment (2015)

"Arriving at the depths of despair as a result of multiple TBIs as an Army Green Beret, Andrew Marr hit rock bottom, mentally and emotionally. Andrew and Adam Marr share their journey as brothers so others on the same path will know there are true, physiologic underlying reasons for the spiral downward and a path back to health. Their book is about hope: that it's possible to determine one's own outcome, no matter how dark the future appears. If you have a loved one suffering the effects of war, read this book now. Seek the wisdom and experience from those who have been to hell and back. "

– Michael Lewis, MD, MPH, MBA, FACPM, FACN
Colonel (Retired), U.S. Army
Author, *When Brains Collide: What every athlete and parent should know about the prevention and treatment of concussions and head injuries*
www.WhenBrainsCollide.com

"Andrew Marr has written a moving, gritty, unembellished account of a long and formidable struggle. In the wake of a series of multiple traumatic brain injuries that cost him nearly everything, he found his way out—and largely flying solo at that. This book may just make him even more valuable to other victims and their families than he was as a Special Forces Green Beret."

– Martin Polanco, MD
Founder and CEO of Crossroads Ibogaine Treatment Center

"Special Operations soldiers are driven by "why" and "how." When a challenge is presented, they search for a deep understanding of "why" the issue is occurring. With that understanding, they develop and test every possible "how" to meet a challenge. *Tales from the Blast Factory* exemplifies the special operations mentality to solve any problem through persistence, understanding, and teamwork. An excellent read for those searching to find solutions for those affected by traumatic brain injury."

– Matthew Griffin

Army Ranger
Combat Flip Flops Co-Founder and CEO
www.combatflipflops.com

"Andrew Marr conveys clearly the connection between hormones and overcoming TBI/PTSD. Our hormones have a much stronger impact on how we think and feel than how we think and feel affects our hormones. Andrew is at the forefront of explaining why everyone with PTSD should have their hormonal profile tested as it could very well be the overlooked reason for your symptoms."

– Mike Mahler

Author of *Live Life Aggressively! What self-help gurus should be telling you*
Co-Host of the Live Life Aggressively Podcast
http://www.mikemahler.com/

"As a senior strategic and administrative operations leader, I have worked around the globe in some of the most challenging locations and environments. But almost nothing compares to the challenges Andrew has faced and overcome in his painstaking return from the brink. I recommend this book to anyone and everyone who has mountains to climb—no matter what form they take."

– Joshua Katz

Army Ranger, Senior CIA Operative, Counter-Terrorism Expert
Warrior Angels Foundation Board Member
Former Senior Policy Advisor to the House Committee on Homeland Security

"This book has something to say about the treatment of our heroes and what can be done for them that isn't currently being done. Think about putting your life on the line every day. You don't, they do. Andrew Marr brilliantly tells the story of the journey of the Warrior Angel. I recommend it to those who want insight and help."

– Michael I. Levy

Hollywood Film Producer
Partner in Falcon6

TALES FROM THE BLAST FACTORY

TALES FROM THE
BLAST
FACTORY

*A Brain Injured Special Forces Green
Beret's Journey Back From the Brink*

ADAM MARR AND ANDREW MARR

NEW YORK

LONDON • NASHVILLE • MELBOURNE • VANCOUVER

TALES FROM THE BLAST FACTORY

*A Brain Injured Special Forces Green Beret's Journey
Back From the Brink*

Published in New York, New York, by Morgan James Publishing. Morgan James is a trademark of Morgan James, LLC. www.MorganJamesPublishing.com

The Morgan James Speakers Group can bring authors to your live event. For more information or to book an event visit The Morgan James Speakers Group at www.TheMorganJamesSpeakersGroup.com.

ISBN 9781683504948 paperback
ISBN 9781683504955 eBook
Library of Congress Control Number: 2017903908

Cover Design by:
Rachel Lopez
www.r2cdesign.com

Interior Design by:
Chris Treccani
www.3dogdesign.net

In an effort to support local communities, raise awareness and funds, Morgan James
Publishing donates a percentage of all book sales for the life of each book to
Habitat for Humanity Peninsula and Greater Williamsburg.

Get involved today! Visit
www.MorganJamesBuilds.com

TABLE OF CONTENTS

DEDICATION

For Becky. My wife, soul mate, and the love of my life.

You are unconditional love.

Every day married to you is a honeymoon.

Our life is heaven on earth.

FOREWORD

'm neither a fatalist nor a believer in divine intervention, but I do believe in the chaos theory. It's a theory in which so many random events are going on in and around us, it becomes difficult to predict with any certainty what will happen next. This summarizes the manner in which I met Green Beret Special Forces Operator James "Andrew" Marr. And chaos or otherwise, it was a very good thing.

As a family-practice physician who was drawn to endocrinology and then neuroendocrinology— the science of the ductless glands (thyroid, adrenals, testes, ovaries) that make hormones— studying their influence on the brain held me hostage the way dark chocolate does. I couldn't get enough.

The randomness that led Andrew to me, and me to him, came about through his relentless pursuit of answers to his medical challenges. This included the fact that he was on thirteen different medications, some of them mind-altering narcotics, none of which provided relief from the deep depression, unpredictable rage, extreme mood swings, suicidal thoughts, and other unbearable conditions that suffused his days and nights. He drank to endure, but he could not escape himself. Repeatedly exposed to blast waves throughout multiple deployments, as well as being knocked unconscious by a massive explosion associated with a weapons cache on his last rotation, the robust, respected career Green Beret had emerged a shadow of himself.

Though considered one of the "lucky ones" who never lost an arm or leg, the damage was much deeper and more insidious. This is commonly referred to as the "silent wound" or "stealth wound" of the Gulf War, Iraq, and Afghanistan. The condition actually had its roots in wars that preceded it, where returning soldiers were labeled "shell-shocked." Too many of our soldiers today are walking around on a multitude of medications, but are still broken and unable to readjust to civilian life. They take their own lives as a final solution at a rate of over twenty-two per day since the medical community has failed to come up with something other than symptom masking.

Somehow, on a chosen day, at a chosen moment, Andrew and I connected. He was desperate to be fixed so he could continue to be a son to his parents; a brother to his brothers; a husband to his beautiful wife, Becky; and a father to their five children. He feared more the possibility that one of his children would stumble onto his lifeless body one afternoon when he just couldn't take it anymore, joining the ranks of the twenty-two per day.

I was eager to apply the treatment protocols we had been working on for more than twenty years in the veterans' community. These protocols were to address post traumatic brain injury hormonal deficiency syndrome, which Andrew had.

Andrew came into the office and had his initial comprehensive neurosteroids and neuroactive steroids assessment. We subsequently found he was well below the optimal physiological levels for most of the hormones that regulate psychological, physiological, and physical well-being. No wonder he had fallen apart.

Reviewing his past medical history, present medical treatment (which had largely failed him), and complaints of extreme psychological issues, we did a Testosterone Challenge Test: a provocative test that lets us know what to expect from his labs and, more importantly, how he would respond to replenishment of testosterone. A dearth of that hormone, which is responsible for normal brain and body function on so many levels, is among the serious fallout from a traumatic brain injury. Soon after, following the administering of testosterone, Andrew reported he'd "felt like Cinderella for sixty hours" before the effects of the testosterone treatment started to wear off. It was clear we were on the right track.

At present, he has been on his treatment protocol of testosterone and other hormones for two years, and has attained significant emotional and cognitive improvements that have essentially brought him back to life. Tantamount to that, he is off all medications and no longer needs to drink alcohol to control his negative thoughts. I have watched a damaged human being return to the vigorous, loving, productive individual he and his family, friends, and fellow Green Berets used to know. He and his brother, former Army Captain Adam Marr, have cofounded the Warrior Angels Foundation, with the conviction that thousands of veterans (and others) with TBIs needn't lead painful, hopeless, debilitated lives, the way he did, because of inappropriate and/or failed medical treatments.

In struggle and suffering, if we're open to them, there are spiritual awakenings that impact each of us, not just injured veterans. Andrew acknowledged and met his challenges head on, finding the kind of inspiration that comes from the worst of circumstances if we just remember that from every bad there comes a greater good and we can decide how to apply that good.

From Andrew, I learned about a valuable tool he'd used in the darkest of times, something he said he'd had in his heart and mind before his first deployment, called up often, and eventually written down for himself and his children. It's his **Standard of Performance**, which follows. It served in war, and continues to serve in civilian life, as a constant compass for him when everything else goes awry: a reminder of what it is to love, contribute, and perform to the very best of one's abilities—to make and be the difference in the world.

Mark L. Gordon, MD
Medical Director
Millennium Health Centers, Inc.
Millennium-WAF TBI Project
CBS Studios
The Clinical Application of Interventional Endocrinology (2007)
Traumatic Brain Injury: A Clinical Approach to Diagnosis and Treatment (2015)

PREFACE

This book does not glorify combat. It is not a combat memoir or a chronologically accurate description of my combat experiences. In some places, timelines are condensed and events, merged to maintain operational security and to better illuminate lessons learned. This book provides the reader with principles and practical applications to create an elevated internal state that is greater than the external environment, to thrive on life's many battlefields.

Before I was ever in a life-and-death situation, I'd already decided what I was going to do when confronted with one. The most important questions in life must be anticipated—with ready answers—before they occur. In situations of life and death, there is no time to pause, reflect, and contemplate a response. Defaulting to one's own foundational level of training is imperative.

As a Special Forces Green Beret, it was important for me to understand the risks. The stakes were not just my life or my family members' lives if I made the wrong choices and didn't survive, but the lives of the men to the left and right of me as well. Knowing that my team and their families were depending on me to do my job was all the motivation I ever needed.

The Army's Special Forces puts its candidates through a rigorous assessment and selection process. For the few who are selected, this process and subsequent years of training cultivate a specific type of individual with a particular commitment: a commitment to die.

The warrior few are bound by a code. A shared commitment and purpose are found in teams whose code and mission are perfectly aligned. The commitment to die is the ultimate form of love, strange as it may sound. It's a love for all we have trained for, bled for, and overcome along the way. Every last man's decision to fully commit produces immeasurable self-confidence and strength. The team must know that when the time comes, and it *will* come, no self-reflection or contemplation is required. The commitment to act and sacrifice was made long before the soldier ever set foot on the battlefield, and there is real liberation in it: the freedom to live, serve, and love without fear of failure or dying.

Warriors are united by an indelible bond, enabling us to operate effectively from the razor's edge. There is power in knowing that all move as you move, all think as you think, and as a cohesive unit with a powerful shared goal, each compensates for another in the places he or she may come up short. These unbreakable bonds are forged in and from united experiences in combat. In Special Forces, we call it "The Brotherhood."

The battlefield is a place of unconditional trust and unquestionable sacrifice. It is its own world. It's where our thoughts sometimes go when we are physically in one place, but we know we really belong in another. It pulls us back.

The duty to my team led to the contemplation of my roles as a husband, father, and leader. I understood there would be times I'd be faced with challenging situations in difficult circumstances. I wrote my **Standard of Performance** to serve as a guide about how to live, love, contribute, and perform to the very best of my abilities—to make and *be* the difference. My combat experiences mandated that I'd default to my most basic level of training when confronted with issues of life and death. My **SoP** would serve as a blueprint for the difficult questions.

As a Special Forces demolitions expert, I was in and around countless explosions. A career spent enduring concussive blast after concussive blast finally caught up with me. I began to suffer the effects of what we now know were multiple "minor" traumatic brain injuries—minor only because they did not put me in the hospital as an injury to the rest of my body may, so it was hard to understand what had actually happened. The "invisible" TBIs sustained in combat led to my medical retirement from the Army—circumstances that included the deeply affecting mental and physical manifestations of TBIs—derailing my life almost to the point of death. Called a signature wound of war, had I not had an **SoP** in place, the fallout from all the TBIs would have caused me to take matters into my own hands, probably ending my life, as the wounds of war do and have done for so many service members and veterans.

As a result of my injuries, I became plagued by depression, angry outbursts, anxiety attacks, mood swings, memory loss, inability to concentrate, learning disabilities, sleep deprivation, loss of libido and lean muscle mass, chronic pain, and alcoholism. I developed a massive deep vein thrombosis—a blood clot that traveled and broke off into both lungs, called a "bilateral pulmonary embolism"—and a number of other medically documented conditions. My drinking was so out of control that my wife, Becky, nine months pregnant with our fifth child, asked me if I could hold it in abeyance for just one day in case she went into labor and couldn't drive herself to the hospital. Things only got worse from there.

While dealing with all of this, I was still trying to come to terms with my medical retirement: the fact that due to my multiple TBIs, I'd been told I could no longer be a Special Forces operator. When you live for the battlefield—and who you are inside is indistinguishable from that role—it can feel as though your life is over. It certainly did for me. Being a Special Forces Green Beret was my whole identity. I was careening into a permanent state of purposelessness—hopelessness—with no way out.

I recall being at my son's hospital bedside after he'd developed a life-threatening medical issue, popping another Dilaudid (an opioid pain medication), chased by another airplane bottle of whiskey, which I'd surreptitiously dumped into a can of Coke Zero. And this was at a time I'd already gone through multiple military medical programs designed to help me manage my TBI condition. Aside from drifting between purposelessness and hopelessness, keeping myself in a chemically altered state was the reason I got up each morning. *That* had become my purpose. *But one day it was different.* I looked at my son and told myself, *All right, this is going to go one of two ways.* I could continue to blame the course conventional medicine had laid out for me—a steep, jagged cliff I climbed each day with a tub of alcohol and, eventually, a backpack of mind-altering narcotics and other heavy meds—which was setting me up for death and the destruction of my family. Or I could embrace my pain—channel it correctly—and act on it to improve my situation. From that moment on, I chose the latter. I made an immutable decision not to give external objects and obstacles power over me. I called upon a newfound focus to change what I didn't like about my current condition: everything. From that time on, I understood the power of choice—that I had it in me to decide how I would receive, process, and respond to external circumstances in my life. It was an epiphany. The shackles were gone. I was back on the battlefield, where I'd felt the most comfortable, confident, and in control, but this time, instead of committing to die, I was committing to live.

I've always subscribed to the tenet that if you don't like something, fix it. When I'd reached out for help, the course of action the conventional medical profession had taken, through the military, fixed nothing and, in fact, was destroying my family and me. Our quality of life was unbearable. The health care I was receiving was a series of mind-bending Band-Aids that definitely were not treating the underlying condition. It masked symptoms and exacerbated problems. I told myself I was done with all of it: I was going out in search of a way to heal myself.

* * * *

Years of experience in this realm have shown me that it's the space between stimuli and response where our battles are won or lost. As I said in the beginning, the most important questions in life must be anticipated—with ready answers—before they occur. In situations of life or death (and in other forms of crises), there is no time to pause, reflect, and contemplate a response. Defaulting to one's own foundational level of training is imperative. In this book, I share the principles and tools that saved my life, launched me on a path to start a foundation to help others in similar conditions when all doors seem closed. The events, lessons learned, and practical applications provided were paid for in blood. When all hope seemed lost, the principles outlined in the coming pages served to illuminate my alternative path. Those who apply the principles will be empowered to create their own way, regardless of circumstance.

The Warrior Angel is a brave and experienced fighter of exemplary virtue. The Warrior Angel believes in doing the right thing, not for promise of reward or fear of reprisal, but because it's the right thing to do. This is the Way of the Warrior Angel.

De Oppresso Liber
Andrew Marr, cofounder and CEO
Warrior Angels Foundation
#UntilThereAreNone

MY STANDARD OF PERFORMANCE

*"If you can meet with Triumph and Disaster
And treat those two imposters just the same . . ."*
—Rudyard Kipling, *"If"*

The real measure of life is how the race is run. Triumph and disaster are only by-products. To run the best race, one must cultivate a process in which a laser-sharp focus results in the capacity to plan, prepare, and perform to the best of one's abilities.

British philosopher and author James Allen wrote, "A man is literally what he thinks, his *character* being the *complete sum of all* his thoughts." Whether you believe that you can or that you can't, you're right. You cannot control what happens to you in life, but you can control what you will feel and do about what happens, and so, in one way or another, you can shape your circumstances.

In his book *Man's Search for Meaning,* neurologist and psychiatrist Viktor E. Frankl said that our primary motivation in this life is our personal search for meaning. His experience as an inmate of a concentration camp was the catalyst for his discovery of meaning in all forms of existence—even the most horrific. History reveals the presence of a relentless search for meaning amidst great tragedy, suffering, genocide, and more.

If you have a big enough "why," you will always find the "how." A conscious effort to perform at one's best in all things at all times in the pursuit of meaning yields unlimited opportunity and fulfillment.

Furthermore, I believe purpose and fulfillment are ultimately realized through love and how we give to others. In this way, placing others' needs ahead of our own in consistent acts of selflessness provides for the kind of meaning and success we can only begin to imagine. When things become hopeless, and even when they are not, find a way to make what you do about somebody else.

—Andrew Marr, 2013

INTRODUCTION

By Adam Marr

I served my country honorably, accomplished incredible goals among incredible people who were doing the same, and came out a decade later relatively unscathed. My injuries were not debilitating in the context of my brother, Andrew's, journey, and in the plight of so many others. But it is enormously important to share how one person's struggles can affect his or her inner circle—specifically, family. I was deeply affected by Andrew's physical and emotional pain and suffering. Similarly, it is important to ascertain what a family member can provide amid a loved one's efforts to navigate these challenging circumstances.

In the summer of 2006, just prior to the 2007 surge in Iraq that increased the number of troops sent over, I graduated from college and left for Fort Rucker in Alabama to attend helicopter flight school. A little more than two years later, I was at Fort

Riley, Kansas, as a newly minted AH-64D Apache helicopter pilot with my fiancée, Alycia. My brother and I would each become ordained and certified online, and then officiate at one another's wedding ceremonies within twelve months. Interestingly, it all began as an elaborate joke that turned into a dare, and neither one of us backed down. There was no question we were close. Following my wedding in 2009, I would go on to hold positions as platoon leader, battle captain, assistant S-3, and company commander. I also made pilot-in-command and air mission commander.

I deployed to Operation Iraqi Freedom/Operation New Dawn. My company, along with my copilot/gunner and I, qualified as the top guns in the battalion. We surpassed two other companies for the unit award and over forty other aircrews for the top honors. I was fortunate enough to be in command of some of the best pilots and crew chiefs in the Army when my company was selected to be the first to field, qualify on, train, and validate the new AH-64E Apache helicopter.

When I laced up my boots for the last time, I still had my limbs and my mental faculties. But many came out the other side a shell of the person they had been. They suffered the effects of war physically, mentally, emotionally, or some combination of all three. If you were lucky enough to survive the experience without being affected by one of these, then you surely know someone who wasn't as fortunate. Perhaps it was someone in your battalion, your company, your platoon, or your squad. But it wasn't you. It's not your story, though it doesn't mean you were not affected. It doesn't mean you are not part of *the* story.

Where I'm concerned, it wasn't someone in my unit. It wasn't someone on my deployment. It wasn't even someone at my duty station. It was someone much closer to home than that. Indeed, Andrew is my brother in arms, but also my brother by birth.

The impact a big brother has is huge. Writer Cameron Gray once summarized my brother this way: "There are some people that, when you see them, you know they served in the military. They have a certain look, a way of composing themselves. Andrew Marr is one of those men. Tall, muscular, and imposing, when you shake his hand, you try not to wince from the strength of his grip. Upon meeting him, before he even says a word, you know he means business."[1]

While Gray surely nailed his physical presence, what he didn't convey was Andrew's innate ability to achieve—to excel at the highest levels of any task to which he commits. But that level of performance was not something that simply

---

1 www.opportunitylives.com/warrior-angels-foundation-makes-strides-treating-traumatic-brain-injuries/

appeared when he became a Green Beret; it's been inside him for as long as I can remember.

Maybe it started in the fourth grade when Andrew wasn't hustling enough in peewee football practice, much to our father's disappointment. The result: Dad made him run home from practice alongside the driver's window—in full pads—for two miles. Mom was not happy, to say the least, and I think Dad came out the worse for wear after that one, far worse than Andrew, anyway. But from that point on, Andrew had the best hustle on the entire team, be it practice, game, or playoffs! Dad may have driven home the point, but Andrew always had it in him. No one has ever questioned his hustle since.

Life always seemed harder for Andrew than for me. It isn't that he wasn't capable, but it seemed to throw him more curveballs—more adversity. Still, he'd go on to win two high school football state championships. One was as a freshman in 1996 when he was called up to the varsity team for the playoffs, and the second was in 1998 as a two-way starting varsity defensive-offensive lineman. In his senior year, the team was an early season favorite to make another deep run in the playoffs, considered back-to-back contenders. Andrew and many of his teammates were being courted by most Division I colleges. However, his senior team was riddled with key injuries to several star players early in the season, and Andrew was unable to escape the fate. In addition to the "normal" bumps to the head that most, if not all, football players experience, he fractured his leg above the ankle during practice, ending his football season and his high school playing career, as well as—we assumed—putting an end to his chances of being recruited on a college football scholarship.

Around this time, Andrew considered entering the military to pursue his other childhood passion: the United States Army Special Forces. But he put it on the back burner to design and execute his own rehabilitation, ultimately receiving a football scholarship to Blinn College in Brenham, Texas. Because he had the vision to break down the problem into manageable steps and the discipline to follow through, his commitment eventually led to a Division II football scholarship at Texas A&M University–Kingsville, where he completed his degree. Although I'm two years his junior, we ended up graduating from college at about the same time. This was largely because of his long rehabilitation and recovery, and also due to his painstaking effort to overcome the challenges of almost every school telling him that as a result of his injury, they were no longer interested in recruiting him.

Graduating college before Andrew was one of the few times in my life I arrived at a destination before he did. He has always been physically stronger, and I believe that his mental prowess was stronger than mine at the time. I'm not sure I'd have come out on top as many times as he did in the early days. In hindsight, I attribute so much of my own **SoP** to my brother. As are a lot of little brothers, I was in an endless competition to surpass him—to be better than he was. *He was in an endless competition with himself—to be the best version of himself.* I still have that competition in me, but as I learned from Andrew, my focus now lies in becoming *the best version of myself.* I believe he was unwittingly teaching me how to set goals, overcome obstacles, and meet seemingly insurmountable challenges. He taught me that even in the deepest valleys of adversity and despair, when everyone tells you it can't be done, it's only what you tell yourself and do about it that ultimately matters.

When Andrew returned from Afghanistan after he'd suffered his latest and most significant traumatic brain injury, the one that actually knocked him unconscious (we'd later learn that a TBI can occur without losing consciousness, and Andrew had sustained many), his downward spiral was full bore. I would find myself on the other end of the phone, increasingly concerned and extremely confused—confused about how my older brother, a mountain of a man both physically and mentally, could go from the pinnacle of success to the depths of self-destruction. From my perspective, this is the story of a family member watching his larger-than-life older brother charge toward an early grave. It's observing all the signs and symptoms of someone crying out for help, for answers, for understanding, for relief, and his being utterly helpless if not, ultimately, for the preparation and training that had taught him to persevere and the decisions he'd made when he entered the service about how he'd handle life-and-death situations. At the point I'm talking about, Andrew was as close to death as anyone I'd ever known.

This book is not written for accolades, nor is it written for critics or naysayers. It's more personal than that. Our intention is to share our journey so that others walking the same path will understand it's possible to prepare and equip themselves to determine their own outcomes, no matter what.

When you learn how to navigate life's challenges, you're free. This book should serve as your compass, helping you blaze a path that previously would have been unattainable. From there, a life bursting with purpose, meaning, passion, and fulfillment is yours for the making.

Adam Marr, cofounder
Warrior Angels Foundation

CHAPTER 1

The Grind of Combat

I joined the Army in a post-9/11 era with no preconceived notions about what I was signing up to do. Nobody can truly comprehend combat until they've been in it, but regardless of its risks, that's where I wanted to be. Much to my parents' chagrin, I decided to enlist in lieu of commissioning as an officer. My brother, Adam, who commissioned as an officer after college, tried to urge me to go to Officer Candidate School as well. I wanted to be an operator, and I knew my time on the teams would be short-lived had I gone the commissioned route. I considered the idea momentarily, but it was not for me. I was a leader regardless of the rank I wore on my chest.

When I enlisted, that's all I saw myself doing: being in the trenches. And because I loved my job, I became exceptional at it. I was well respected; I loved the people I got to be around; I loved the common cause. I embraced the level of commitment it took to execute tasks at that level and I respected the courage it required from the men to my left and right. I was surrounded 24/7, 365 with men of the same mind-set who, in turn, made me raise my game to another level. Bringing anything less than my "A" game was unthinkable. The consequences could be fatal.

I'd found a home in combat. Leaving my team and that way of life—the way of the warrior—was as foreign a concept to me as breathing without oxygen. The brotherhood and the grind of combat became like air, food, and water. I couldn't live without it. I was sure it was my purpose—that I was born to it. Lead men into battle; kill evil; free the oppressed. I thought I'd do it forever, or until someone told me I couldn't anymore. I just didn't realize it would happen so soon. No one ever does.

Combat withstanding, this was an era before the superabundance of information that has come out in very recent years about the inherent brain dangers from football on any level: Pop Warner, high school, college, or professional. A study from the University of Texas Southwestern Medical Center's Peter O'Donnell Jr. Brain Institute and

Wake Forest University School of Medicine showed that "Repeated impacts to the heads of high school football players cause immeasurable changes in their brains, even when no concussion occurs . . ."[2] Between my football years and my military duties, the damage was mounting.

By definition, aftereffects of a head injury include being dazed or unaware of where you are—what we call "getting your bell rung." Seeing stars and ringing in your ears are also symptoms many individuals who work in and around explosives experience. Among my roles on the team was that of master breacher, tasked with creating the explosive charges put on doors, windows, and other points of entry from which we'd have to get a "safe" distance away and then blow up the device and go back inside. It's hard to quantify precisely, but the number of TBIs I've received in my life is in the double, if not triple, digits.

In retrospect, every time we executed one of those blasts, no matter how small, everyone was at risk of, and may have sustained, a TBI. The fact is, I'd done hundreds if not thousands of explosives charges over the course of my career, but that's the life of an operator. The only time I

2 "Single season of contact sports can cause measurable brain changes." Medical News. April 26, 2016. http://www.news-medical.net/news/20160426/Single-season-of-contact-sports-can-cause-measurable-brain-changes.aspx

was ever knocked unconscious was on a mission in 2013, and it was brief. That's why for so many months after I'd completed what was to be my last deployment, there were no correlations made between repeated head traumas and the slow but sure cognitive, emotional, behavioral, and physical decline and nightmare for me that followed.

* * * *

Whiskey. **A**lpha. **R**omeo. **D**elta. **A**lpha. **K**ilo. The last place I deployed to in Afghanistan is called Wardak Province, located in the central east region. I had to spell it out because it's not a place most people know. It is marked by the Kabul—Kandahar Highway, maybe a little better identified, though most of Wardak's half a million residents live in remote villages. At that point, though, we were in the capital: Maidan Shahr. It was infested with free-roaming enemies terrorizing the local populace. The Taliban enjoyed total freedom of movement, walking openly in public while heavily armed. They were the law. We were tasked with clearing them out. The engagements that ensued resulted in the most violent combat of my SF career.

On June 3, 2013, we were going after a known facilitator of improvised explosive devices—commonly known as IEDs—in an attempt to capture or kill him. The following excerpt was taken from my Purple Heart denial appeal (addressed in Chapter 7), recounting the specifics of the engagement:

> On ▮▮▮▮▮▮ 2013, ODA xxxx to include Sergeant First Class (SFC) Marr, was part of an operation in ▮▮▮▮▮▮▮▮▮▮ Wardak Province, Afghanistan, with their Afghan National Army Special Forces (ANASF) counterparts. Their Afghan-led mission was to investigate a suspected insurgent weapons cache. Once at the suspected cache, SFC Marr's team strong pointed the compound while their ANASF counterparts entered the compound. SFC Marr's team entered the compound after the ANASF asked for support. The compound was clear of insurgent and civilian personnel. During the sensitive site exploitation, a hole containing what was believed to be 107mm rockets was identified. During the investigation of the munitions, SFC Marr found anti-tampering devices attached to the rockets. Upon notification of the anti-tampering devices, the ODA's team sergeant ordered all nonessential personnel to evacuate the compound. Once all nonessential personnel were clear of the site, SFC Marr and his 18C (Special Forces

Engineer) counterpart began to prep charges to explosively reduce the cache site. The team received a heavy volume of effective PKM (Soviet-made machine gun), small arms (AK 47 automatic rifle), and RPG (rocket propelled grenade) fire as the ODA's team sergeant was setting up an outside perimeter.

SFC Marr and team were pinned down by the effective enemy PKM, small arms, and RPG fire at a cover and concealed position that was within 50M of the cache site. SFC Marr and team would have to cross the cache site and an open danger area to link back up with their main element. The enemy continued to place accurate RPG fire directed at the cache site. One effective RPG round would have triggered the explosives to a sympathetic discharge (a blast wave from one munition can ignite other nearby munitions). SFC Marr and team's current position made link up with the main element tactically unfeasible and would have resulted in multiple US casualties from the effective enemy RPG fire. SFC Marr detonated the explosives, resulting in a documented TBI. The exact contents of the cache were unknown; however, the battle space owner 3rd Infantry Division Intelligence Section estimated the cache due to size of blast and human intelligence to have contained approximately 12 107mm rockets.

An attempt to move to a friendly position while the cache site was in danger of a sympathetic discharge while being pinned down by effective enemy fire made SFC Marr and team's movement tactically unfeasible. Not detonating the explosives would've resulted in the team being vulnerable without a covered and concealed position ensuing in catastrophic US fatalities. The enemy situation dictated SFC Marr's decision to detonate. SFC Marr's actions under effective enemy fire allowed the team to effectively break contact, fight back to their main element, resulting in no US or ANASF casualties while reducing a known enemy cache site. SFC Marr received a medical retirement on 28 June 2015 from wounds received in combat.

The next things I remember after detonating the cache are the sound of glass breaking and my being completely engulfed in extreme blackness. I came to, prone, on my stomach, having no idea where I was because the sun had been swallowed up by the debris from the blast. I put my hands over my head because I somehow thought I was inside a building that was collapsing on me. I felt the area all around and realized I was not inside, but I was unsure of why the sun, which had just been shining, was now blotted out. We began taking more machine gun fire, which turned a switch back on inside of me as I realized we were definitely still fighting. My teammates and I were able to fight back, and much later, in making sense of what had happened with all of my symptoms, it was clear I'd suffered one of many TBIs. It would take many, many months before correlations were made between what happened that day and the cascade of physical, emotional, and behavioral issues that ensued for me. We laid low for a few days, and after that, it was back to the blast factory.

* * * *

On June 8, just five days later, we were back out on the hunt. My wife, Becky, who was about eight months pregnant with our first son, was home with our three daughters. It was understood that I'd go home for the birth and then attend Delta Force assessment and selection, keeping me stateside for the last half of that deployment. Within minutes of our arrival on the objective, we began taking enemy fire. Two team guys quickly came under accurate sniper fire and were pinned down at their location. They'd remain at their covered-and-concealed position in the kill zone until we could get them out.

The new mission was to neutralize the threat and get them out of the kill zone. The enemy sniper team was up on a mountain, with what we determined were several enemy combatants, so we could not effectively move to them. That left us with the option to engage with our organic weapon systems in the hope we could get the enemy to put their heads down long enough to get our guys out of there. We got some air on station, an Air Force A-10 Warthog Close-Support fixed-wing aircraft. The entire airframe is designed around its beautiful and destructive thirty-millimeter cannon: a cannon that saved our lives on more than one occasion. The A-10 effectively neutralized the enemy. Once we got our men back, we loaded up the vehicles to return to base—when further disaster struck.

I always traveled in the back of the lead vehicle. I did this because I needed to be the first one out to investigate and reduce any IEDs we came across. We were in a convoy of about a half-dozen RG vehicles (a mine-resistant light armored vehicle). I was in the lead vehicle in the back of the RG next to the bombproof exit door and window. We were riding with about one hundred meters between each vehicle when the one behind us hit an IED. I recall looking back and seeing the entire vehicle shoot up about twenty feet in the air. It seemed like slow motion, but then the forty-two-thousand-pound vehicle came crashing down on its side. From past occurrences, I knew the magnitude of what had happened to the occupants, though we could not simply dismount from the other RGs and rush to their aid. We had to be exceedingly cautious of our movements around other prospective IEDs and enemy fire. We also realized as soon as the explosion took place that the enemy was probably initiating an ambush. Very carefully, we closed the distance to the disabled RG, finding the blast had blown off the front passenger door. The teammate who'd been in the front seat was actually now trapped underneath the vehicle and unconscious. The vehicle's gun, positioned at three o'clock had actually prevented him from being crushed by the fallen vehicle. Had it been at two o'clock or four o'clock, he would have died.

Four others in the RG were also severely injured, and as we started to work on trying to free our trapped teammate, the enemy began its ambush. AK, machine gun, and RPG fire began to rain down on us. I took some of our guys and some Afghan Special Forces guys to set up a security perimeter.

The landing zone was too hot at that time to land a medevac (a helicopter used to remove sick or injured people from an area). We orchestrated

A-10 Close Air Support, or CAS, gun run after gun run on multiple enemy locations. Hours later, we finally got a medevac in to take the wounded out to higher echelons of care. The fight grew fiercer after the medevac departed, and we had to call for reinforcements. When all was said and done, thousands of pounds of bombs were accurately placed on multiple enemy locations.

We needed to investigate the blast site that had overturned the RG to figure out from what point the IED had been initiated. There was a lull in enemy fire after the gun runs, but no one would be dumb enough to stick around after all that carnage was unleashed from the sky, or so I thought. My teammate and I alerted the rest of the team that we were going to see if we could gather any intel from the suspected IED initiation site. We walked head-on into another near-ambush about one hundred meters away from the building that we thought had been where the blast initiated. Once again, the enemy opened up from a tree line about 150 meters away with RPG, AK, and PKM machine gun fire. Luckily for us, they were not too accurate with their fire this time. Without communicating, my teammate and I defaulted into a choreographed protocol of one man engaging and laying down covering fire while the other man would bound back several feet, get set, and then start laying down covering fire for the other man to bound back. This process is repeated until both are out of the kill zone. It is a thing of beauty that had become second nature to us by now. We got back and called for more CAS on that location. It wasn't tactically feasible to do a proper battle damage assessment, but the number of enemy killed and wounded was significant.

With the injured gone, we now had three fewer men from my team in the fight. They would not operate for the rest of the deployment. After seeing my vehicle blown up and assessing the damage to my teammates at the blast site, I made a instant decision to forgo returning home for the birth of my son who was due in a few weeks. I had to stay with my team and finish the job. Becky and my children were safe. They were cared for and provided for. They had shelter. They had running water. Air-conditioning. Indoor plumbing. Refrigeration. Hospitals nearby. No threat of imminent danger. In our position, we had none of the above. I knew my soon-to-be-born son would appreciate that decision when he was old enough to comprehend it. Becky's response was reassuring.

She said, "Baby, we all love you and are so proud of you. You do whatever you have to do to bring the rest of those boys back home alive and safe. We'll all be here waiting for you when you get back."

I was confident in my team and I was confident in my skill and experience level, but I also knew there was a high probability that I wouldn't make it back alive. We were walking the razor's edge and we all knew it.

CHAPTER 2

A Cry for Help

I returned home from Afghanistan in August 2013, a few weeks ahead of my team. I met my son, Jace, for the first time at the Sea-Tac Airport baggage claim. In the weeks and months that followed, things began to change for me. The only thing I was sure of was that I was different. I couldn't put my finger on it; I was just off. The deployment had been emotionally and physically taxing on the whole team. I decided we'd been grinding for a while, and I thought my body needed a break and then I'd be back to normal.

Like a slow burn, because of the post-traumatic brain inflammation that had stemmed from my multiple TBIs (of which I was completely unaware at that time), my body started to rebel.

Scientific research states the effects of a brain injury can surface on impact—or a long time afterward.[3] It was about three months after my return to the States that I began to notice some changes. I was plagued by depression, angry outbursts, anxiety, mood swings, memory loss, an inability to concentrate, learning disabilities, sleep deprivation, loss of libido and lean body mass, muscular weakness, and more. When I finally reached the breaking point, I was drinking all day, consuming a 750-milliliter bottle of bourbon every night, was on more than a dozen medications including mind-altering narcotics, and had become completely detached and isolated from everyone I loved. The manifestations of dementia became familiar territory to me and those around me. I was sleeping with a handle of whiskey and a loaded shotgun by my bed.

The events that led up to it included severe panic attacks. One of the attacks came on at my unit gym when I became lightheaded and dizzy, with a pounding heart rate. I fought off an impending crying jag. I remember telling myself, *You're a Green Beret; do not lose it and start crying in here.* This was foreign territory to me. I felt sad, lonely, and hopeless; I didn't know what to do. I raced to my team room, hoping some of my guys

3 Traumatic Brain Injury. Mayo Clinic. http://www.mayoclinic. org/diseases-conditions/traumatic-brain-injury/basics/symptoms/con-20029302

were there to offer moral support. Finding no one around, I went straight to the Class 6—a liquor store on base—and purchased a bottle of bourbon.

I had no idea what a panic attack felt like. I'd assumed, rather ignorantly, it was an issue for the mentally weak. I would come to understand it had nothing to do with being mentally weak, but at that point, I was positive I was going insane. The only "logical" reaction I could come up with was to start drinking immediately to decrease the feeling of being wildly out of control that was eating me alive. Stopping it was all I could think about. I got in my truck and started drinking straight from the bottle while driving home. My pre-injury self would never have risked drinking and driving but at that point, I didn't care. The potential consequences of my erratic actions never entered my mind. My mind was short-circuiting. I distinctly remember crying uncontrollably, drinking, driving, and wondering why this was happening to me. I began to behave in ways that I hadn't before.

* * * *

At one point, I got into an altercation at a fast-food restaurant as my family watched from our vehicle. I've included this to illustrate the effects a TBI can have on one's ability to reason. While picking up some food for our kids, I witnessed a man in his late teens or early twenties slam a large drink that appeared to be full on the sidewalk. He then began to curse loudly. That angered me. I told him to pick up the drink and to quit acting like a jackass.

He responded with, "You can go screw yourself. Who is going to make me?"

That was the wrong answer.

I walked up to him and repeated the same line. The next thing I remember was backhanding him across the face, immediately knocking him to the pavement. Next, I picked him up and threw him into a busy street with oncoming traffic. I was being controlled by a dark, screaming rage.

A number of bystanders took offense to my actions and rightly so. Unfortunately, several people in that parking lot attempted to get physical with me in protest. I remember standing over the last guy, who tried to stop me from getting in my car. I looked up as he lay prone on the pavement and in an instant, I made eye contact with my wife who was breastfeeding our newborn. They'd witnessed the whole altercation and were horrified. I had allowed my rage to fuel my actions with disastrous results. I didn't understand at that time why I couldn't respond appropriately to certain situations. Regardless of understanding it or not, I realized that if I didn't get it under control, it was going to kill me, or worse: I might kill someone else.

I have some screws loose, I thought. I have always been an optimistic person, sometimes to the point of being obnoxious. I was now a man divided. Half of me was trying to be positive, using self-talk, as usual, but the positive thoughts and self-talk that had governed my life were now being infiltrated by negativity and uncertainty. The darkness came— and kept coming—against my will. I was in a fight to overcome this newfound depression but found myself succumbing to it. I wanted to know what was happening to me and why. These thoughts started to dominate my existence. Believing you're going crazy takes precedence over any other thoughts. It consumed and exhausted me. I loved my wife, our kids, my job, and my team, but I was depressed and I couldn't understand why. I had no reason to be.

* * * *

Up until this point, I had not been a problem drinker. We drank on the team; it's part of the culture. But I'd never had a problem differentiating that kind of occasional indulgence from maintaining a clean, sober, responsible lifestyle with my family or at work. Now I required alcohol 24/7 just to function.

I sought out our group psychologist for help. I was honest with him about what had been going on. I felt it was important because for the first time ever, it seemed as though I had lost my ability to control my actions and emotions. The essence of what he told me was, *Try not to drink this weekend and because you haven't really slept in four or five months. Try to get some more sleep.*

I was baffled walking out of his office. The next week involved several more panic attacks, which included breaking down uncontrollably at home in front of my family. After not being able to sleep it all off per the psychologist's recommendation to try to get more sleep, I was prescribed a benzodiazepine—a sedative with crushing side effects. My anxiety and depression continued to worsen.

From there, I was sent to the TBI clinic on base and put through a battery of neuropsychological testing. I had a difficult time answering the questions and completing the tasks. I was accused of trying to skew the results to make it look as though I was not trying to perform well; like scheduling a neuropsych test on which to underperform was how I wanted to spend my free time! Waiting for the results of each test from the TBI clinic took two to three additional weeks. Then an appointment would be set up for me yet *another* two or three weeks into the future to discuss the results and try to figure out what to do from there.

At one point, the results of some blood work did indicate I was deficient in certain hormones, including testosterone (a common by-product of TBI). But there was no connection made to TBI or brain inflammation—something that would come out much later in my protracted search for help and answers.

At that time, I was sent to an endocrinologist on base. The endocrinologist, a full-bird colonel, talked to me as though I were wasting his time. I was there because my recent blood work had shown that I was severely deficient in several key hormones. The colonel told me the only physiological explanation for my hormones being so low was the result of abusing anabolic steroids. He told me that my levels were lower than those of one of his patients suffering from a brain tumor. I asked him if any correlations could be made between my symptoms and chronic blast-wave exposure.

All he said was, "No, I have never seen or heard anything like that."

It got pretty ugly from there. I was treated like a heroin or methadone addict, in there for the express purpose of scoring some drugs. The colonel told me he would consider treating me only after I passed a urinary analysis for anabolic steroids. The urinary analysis results would take four to six weeks to come back. I got up and walked off, dismayed by the level of disrespect I'd been shown. All this from a man who couldn't tell the difference between a barrel and a buttstock, much less, point it at the enemy and pull the trigger when the time called for it. The endocrinologist, like the staff at the TBI clinic before him, seemed to think I enjoyed scheduling appointments, sitting in waiting rooms for extended periods of time, divulging highly personal information about how my life was unraveling, in order to be treated like I was making everything up. I started to question my sanity; this level of care was not adding up. As a senior enlisted Special Forces Green Beret, I knew I could fend for myself. What was the eighteen- or nineteen-year-old private in the same situation supposed to do?

At that point, in an effort to "rectify" my hormone deficiency, I was put on sixty milligrams a day of a topical testosterone gel. An adult male in his thirties manufactures about sixty milligrams a *week*, and I was directed to take that amount every day. When you replace testosterone in someone who is shown to be deficient in it, you run the risk of shutting down the precursors to that hormone. That is why it is essential to have a protocol that takes that into account by adding didehydroepiandrosterone (DHEA) and pregnenolone to offset testosterone shutting down those two important precursors. This fact was not implemented in the protocols I was prescribed. This renders the testosterone useless after four to six months of use, the amount of time it takes to shut down the natural production of DHEA and pregnenolone. I was using testosterone but without any benefit.

I was now seeing a different psychologist and endocrinologist, and undergoing continued neurological testing. I was ultimately referred to an endocrinologist at the University of Washington Medical Center, but the short of it is that there was no communication between medical and psychological entities, or medical and other medical entities. No one knew what the other was doing or learning. There was no cooperation—no effort on anyone's part to put one finding together with another. Each doctor was the proverbial island, and I was the one adrift and flailing among all of them.

* * * *

In my increasingly desperate quest to heal, I eventually learned about the National Intrepid Center of Excellence (NICoE) at Walter Reed National Military Medical Center in Bethesda, Maryland. It was comforting to think there might be an answer out there and this could be it. NICoE's purpose, according to its website, is to provide "Hope, Healing, Discovery, and Learning for Traumatic Brain Injury and Psychological Health." My command had never heard of NICoE, and the only reason they were made aware of it is because I brought it to their attention. I took matters into my own hands and managed to get enrolled in their program after I presented the following brief to my battalion command:

WHAT IS A TBI?

- *A TBI is caused by a bump, blow, or jolt to the head or a penetrating head injury that disrupts the normal function of the brain. The severity of a TBI may range from "mild" (i.e., a brief change in mental status or consciousness) to "severe" (i.e., an extended period of unconsciousness or memory loss after the injury).*

SYMPTOMS

- *A TBI can cause a wide range of functional short- or long-term changes affecting thinking, sensation, language, and/or emotions.*
  - *—**Thinking** (i.e., memory and reasoning)*
  - *—**Sensation** (i.e., touch, taste, and smell)*
  - *—**Language** (i.e., communication, expression, and understanding)*

— *Emotion (i.e., depression, anxiety, personality changes, aggression, acting out, and social inappropriateness)*
- *Repeated mild TBIs occurring over an extended period of time (i.e., months, years) can result in cumulative neurological and cognitive deficits. Repeated mild TBIs occurring within a short period of time (i.e., hours, days, or weeks) can be catastrophic or fatal.*

RECOVERY AND TREATMENT
- *Surgery is only needed in extreme cases. For many TBI sufferers, there is medication and alternative medicines that can mitigate symptoms such as headaches, chronic pain, behavioral problems, depression, seizures and chronic pain.*

TBI AND THE PITUITARY
- *Pituitary hormone deficiency may result from head trauma or subarachnoid hemorrhage. Two recent studies show that one or more pituitary hormones may be affected by traumatic brain injury or subarachnoid hemorrhage.*
- *Symptoms of hormone deficiency can mimic other effects of a traumatic brain injury, which can prevent suspicion of this disorder. A deficiency of one or more of the hormones regulated by the pituitary gland may have physical and/or psychological effects such as: reduced muscle*

mass, weakness, decreased exercise capacity, fatigue, irritability, depression, impaired memory, and reduced sex drive.

SECONDARY HYPOGONADISM

- *This type of hypogonadism indicates a problem in the hypothalamus or the pituitary gland — parts of the brain that signal the testicles to produce testosterone. The hypothalamus produces gonadotropin-releasing hormone (GnRH), which signals the pituitary gland to make follicle-stimulating hormone (FSH) and luteinizing hormone (LH). Luteinizing hormone then signals the testes to produce testosterone.*

RECOVERY AND TREATMENT

- *These symptoms can be treated with Hormone Replacement Therapy (HRT).*

OPERATOR STRESS SYNDROME

- *When in a combat environment, a soldier's mental state of alertness and cortisol levels are on high alert the entire time of the deployment. When returning home, the operator will find it difficult to adjust to normal life.*

SYMPTOMS

Fatigue, Irritability, Depression, Difficulty Coping/ Adjusting, Reduced Sex Drive, Difficulty Sleeping

HOW I AM BEING TREATED

- *I am currently being seen by the TBI clinic, an endocrinologist, and a behavioral health specialist.*
- *Each one is only looking at their piece of the pie, so to speak. There is no cross communication between providers.*
- *The average time between each doctor's visit is two and a half weeks at best.*
- *No specialist is looking at this from the point of view that maybe all three are somehow connected.*

MY SYMPTOMS

Erectile Dysfunction, No Sex Drive, Fatigue, Loss of Enthusiasm, Trouble Concentrating, Short-Term Memory Loss, Headaches, Blurry Vision and Double Vision, Balance Issues, Irritability, Trouble Sleeping, Anxiety, Depression, Panic Attacks, Crying for No Reason

- *I feel as if I am going crazy; these symptoms are not me. I had a nervous breakdown and crying attack in front of my wife and kids last Friday. Enough is enough, I have done everything I know to do and nothing seems to be getting better. My depression and panic attacks are only getting worse despite my being placed on antianxiety and antidepressant medications.*

RECOMMENDATIONS

- *I am begging whoever has to make the call to send me to the National Intrepid Center of Excellence*

at Walter Reed in Bethesda, Maryland, to please do so.
- *They have the best specialists and technology in the world to treat soldiers with TBI and BH issues.*
- *My battalion doc, group surgeon, and team leadership are all on board.*
- *NICoE's website is www.nicoe.capmed.mil*
- *I do not want to waste another week knowing that this place exists and I am not there. I do not want to continue to have to put my family through what they are experiencing.*

RECOMMENDATIONS FOR THE GROUP
- *We need to make the guys aware of the link between TBI and hormonal deficiencies, and what these can do to one's behavioral health.*
- *We need the providers to be working as one unit on this matter.*
- *We need to make sure soldiers know exactly where to go to get this help.*
- *We need to educate providers to understand that these symptoms can be caused by multiple external factors, not just one. This will help sufferers to get real answers instead of receiving a temporary Band-Aid over the cut.*
- *We need better testing. The IMPACT test taken upon returning from a trip is total crap. The TBI clinic told me they don't even receive that information.*

- *There needs to be a baseline lab analysis before deployment; if needed, after an injury; another upon return home; and then one every six months.*
- *Again, we must have providers understand that there is some link between TBI, hormonal deficiencies, and out-of-character BH issues.*
- *I think having an annual training on this is more important than sexual-harassment training or some other certification with which teams are bogged down.*
- *I will gladly go team room to team room and talk to guys myself. I know I'm not the only guy having these problems, and I know we can/must/will help our guys if they are suffering.*

* * * *

When I got to NICoE in mid-June 2014, I was relieved to learn there was an interdisciplinary team. Everyone works and communicates with everyone else. That, alone, was a load off my mind. I was also treated with respect and compassion: I was acknowledged and validated as a human being who was genuinely sick, someone proactively and constructively seeking help. NICoE was a four-week program preceded by a detailed application process with acceptance ultimately by invitation. My team included an array of neurologists, endocrinologists, psychologists, neuropsychologists, primary-care physicians— every expert imaginable in the realm of cleaning up the complicated fallout from a TBI.

For the first time, and with NICoE's emphasis as much on education as it is on treatment, I began to comprehend how traumatic brain injuries happen. I learned how explosive blast waves caused shearing (microtears) of neurons in the brain—and how that contributes to the symptoms associated with a TBI. The educational aspect was phenomenal, and I felt that, in that respect, the curtain had been lifted. I learned the term *neuroplasticity:* that the brain is pliable—meaning, it has the capacity to regrow, reorganize, and make new connections so people can teach or reteach themselves how to do things. Even when so much is lost or has changed, as it was and had for me, the brain can be rewired. Broken connections can be repaired. That information was worth its weight in gold. It was a saving grace in almost every way. And yet, with all of this, NICoE's treatment did not address reducing the inflammation or correcting the hormonal deficiencies with which I was left following my head injuries. Instead, it involved the administering of more drugs—some, controlled substances—proclaiming to help me live with what I was told would be my "new normal." It was confusing and disappointing. On the one hand, I felt validated, vindicated, and informed, yet I'd not moved very far along in what would be considered significant recovery from my TBIs. I was told I'd have to learn to endure all the psychological and behavioral issues that had brought me to this point, though with the narcotics and others meds running interference, I just might be able to live with it all. In short, life as I knew it would not be restored. I wasn't sure I was ready to accept this, but it seemed at that juncture, I had no other options.

CHAPTER 3

The War Within

My alcohol consumption spiraled out of control. I began drinking heavily after having returned from my last deployment in the fall of the previous year. I'd gone to NICoE so I could return to my team and operate again. Though my official medical retirement wouldn't happen for quite some time, I'd already felt discharged from life when my group surgeon told me I could not risk sustaining another blow to the head. I was in complete disbelief. My brain was blistering and my insides were churning.

On August 31, 2014, my wife, Becky, nine months pregnant with our second son, asked me to reduce my drinking in case she went into labor and could not drive herself to the hospital. Her request stunned me, but it wasn't enough for me to stop—at least not beyond that day. We were scheduled to pick up my mother-in-law who was flying in for the birth from Texas, and I'd been hobbled by agonizing calf pain for the past three days. The only thing I could think of was that I'd strained it somehow, though I'd tried everything I knew in the realm of stretching, deep breathing, elevating, ice, heat, and more alcohol to alleviate the problem, which only got worse.

I was in so much pain I told Becky I doubted I could make the drive to Sea-Tac International Airport, about 140 miles round-trip. I thought I might need to go to the emergency room. I asked her to drive herself, along with our son, Jace, now nearly fourteen months old. Our three girls would remain home with the eldest, who was entering high school and thus was placed in charge of the younger ones.

Retreating upstairs to lie down, despite my deteriorating physical condition and the fact that I'd felt I'd been going crazy for months, I quickly realized I had to overcome everything—at least for the next few hours. I had to be in charge. I wasn't about to allow my wife, on the verge of delivery, to drive herself and my son that distance. I subsequently worked on myself until I arrived at a mental state where I could push through the pain, as I may have done in combat. Simply put, I had to take care of my family, no matter what.

It was dark by the time we arrived at the airport. Jace was in his car seat, half asleep. He'd been sick for about two weeks with a head cold that had turned into an upper respiratory infection, triggering a build-up of fluids and inflammation in his neck. But it wasn't until we got back into our driveway and began to lift him from the car seat that we observed the scope of the problem: His neck had become noticeably swollen in a short amount of time. Jace had been born with a congenital lymphatic malformation, detected in utero and the size of a kidney bean—cyst-like and close to the surface of his neck. Until now it had not been an issue. But it appeared to be enlarged—the side of his neck resembling a small balloon—and we rushed him to the emergency room at the Madigan Army Medical Center on Joint Base Lewis–McChord.

With Jace in rough condition and the doctors positing it could possibly interfere with his breathing, Becky poised to go into labor, and my leg causing unrelenting pain, we were triaged in the same ER room. I recall getting a shot of Valium to deal with the leg "spasm" as we knew it then. I made it known that my son's health risk was more pressing and my wife could go into an early labor from the stress. Actually, she was beginning to experience contractions, though very far apart.

I hate ERs. You tell your story and then retell it to a multitude of different medical personnel multiple times. I found this to be an inefficient waste of time. And in my mental and physical state, I was not in the mood.

A decision was made to administer intravenous fluids to Jace while awaiting an ear, nose, and throat specialist to check in with us. Of all the horrors I saw in combat, nothing compares to watching your child suffer and for him not to comprehend why. The nurses asked if we wanted to leave the room while they inserted the IV; I replied, "No." I stood over my anxious son on the right side of the bed with my left hand on his chest and my right hand on his forehead. I was bent over so we could look each other in the eye.

The initial stick was unpleasant but not nearly as bad as the next two minutes.

The nurse continued to move the needle around, shaking her head, muttering, "I just can't find it. I just can't find it," referencing his vein.

Watching Jace's reaction just about killed me. He continued to scream every time she moved the needle around. The whites of his eyes got so huge I thought his head was going to burst. I was trying to keep his attention on me. I kept telling him that Daddy was right there, and how tough he was, and how much I loved him. He passed out from the pain.

The nurses figured they would try the other arm. The exact same thing happened. I yelled an obscenity and ordered everyone out in a tone that shook the ER. I was taking no prisoners.

Two minutes later, a nurse from the neonatal intensive care unit showed up with an ultrasound machine. She used the machine to pinpoint his vein and administered the IV that way. It took her about ten seconds to locate the vein and less than that for the IV to be placed gently and safely in place. I was relieved but enraged that my son had been forced to experience what he did with unqualified medical personnel who'd had no business working with babies.

It was now September 1, around three o'clock in the morning. Becky and I were beyond exhaustion; the gravity of what was happening to our son was taking its toll. Jace had been put through the ringer.

The decision was made to admit him and we were moved to pediatrics on the fourth floor. After they got him to his room and hooked up to all his monitors, the nurse told us the doctor would be by in a couple of hours to discuss his treatment. We were told they wanted to monitor his breathing and run some tests to see if the growth in his neck was infected. My poor tough guy looked like he had a potato growing out of the side of his neck.

* * * *

Spasm or otherwise, the pain in my left calf was crippling. I texted my unit doctor, told him the deal, and asked for some Percocet so I could at least function for my family. I was swiftly becoming unable to do so. The doc knew that if I was calling and asking for pain medicine, it was serious and I could not otherwise control it.

He put in the prescription and I left Jace and Becky to go to an off-post pharmacy to pick it up. That's when I decided to start drinking again— as if the idea had ever left my mind. The day for which Becky had asked me to curtail it was over. I pulled over at a gas station and bought a bunch of miniature whiskey bottles and some twenty-ounce Coke Zero bottles. I picked up the narcotic, went back to the hospital, and continued to drink and pop pills to try and kill this fiery pain that was now eating my entire calf.

Becky's contractions were now about five minutes apart. She had been moved to maternity on the second floor while Jace remained on the fourth. I refused any further attention to my leg because I had to take care of my family. I was quite literally yanking it behind me, riding the elevator, and dragging it down corridors to divide my time between both floors. The specialists made a decision to go in surgically and place a drain in Jace's neck with a second objective of taking a closer look inside. Again, despite my own pain, the opiates, and the fact that I'd been secretly consuming alcohol, I made a decision to prepare for three courses of action or COAs: COA 1, COA 2, and COA 3. They involved my mother-in-law, our neighbor Sarah, and some guys from my team. They all helped us out logistically and with their great generosity of spirit. When I repeatedly begged and tried to entice my buddies into bringing me more alcohol at the hospital, they shut it down on the spot.

Two of our three girls, Hailee and Melia, were starting school within a day or so and needed more shopping done; our youngest daughter Ava was just four years old at the time. Transportation had to be finalized, lunches had to be made, and all the other details had to be attended to in order to ensure the girls' smooth transition. Fortunately, my mother-in-law was there, and when she had to be at the hospital, our neighbor—with five children of her own—stepped up to the plate to help care for our daughters.

* * * *

Our second son, Joseph Adam Marr, eight pounds and four ounces, was born on September 2. Jace had to undergo surgery to implant the drain.

Eventually, the doctors talked me into going home to eat, shower, and catch a few hours of sleep, which I did, returning to the hospital as soon as I could. By the time I got back, someone had contacted my medical command to apprise them of the ongoing situation with my leg. They ushered me to radiology, where the image showed a massive deep vein thrombosis—a blood clot. Further imaging revealed it had broken off and traveled to my lungs, where it was diagnosed as a bilateral pulmonary embolism: clots in the lungs that were stopping blood flow. There was a brief window of time to get it all broken up so it wouldn't travel to my brain, causing an aneurism—and even if it didn't, so that I would not risk lack of oxygen and suffer even more brain damage. Becky and tiny JoJo never left the hospital, staying to care for Jace and me. My mother got on her plane and was picked up at Sea-Tac by a teammate. Becky's Facebook post read: *Andrew is admitted now with blood clots in his calf and lungs. At least we're getting things resolved. Thanks to Andrew's team for helping me transport family and for staying with Andrew for hours.*

Jace remained in the hospital, continuing to be monitored with steroids and an antibiotic. The staff didn't want to discharge him for a few more days. We were scheduled to meet with the ear, nose, and throat specialist the following week to discuss a potential treatment called "sclerosis," where they inject fluid into the mass in his neck. The fluid is supposed to dissolve the lymphatic malformation from the inside out. The other option was to go in and cut it out and be done with it, but that procedure would have to be performed at Seattle Children's Hospital, and the Lewis–McChord doctors recommended not operating on Jace unless we absolutely had to. So, OK. We had no reason to question it.

I was discharged on Friday, September 5, early in the morning. I was put on anticoagulants to bring my blood levels down to a therapeutic level. While I was hospitalized, no one ever took the time to explain the first thing about blood clots in general, let alone offer any details. No one thought it important to show me any of the imaging or what to expect in the short term and long term of this new situation. I was struggling to comprehend what was happening. I was, in fact, drugged up, so a detailed explanation may have been too much for me to retain; I understood that. But I expected to be directed to a website or given some form of supportive literature on the situation to read later. Nothing was offered.

In the moments before I was discharged, a doctor provided me with a rapid-fire overview of three different types of blood thinners, how they are administered, and their side effects. He then asked me to choose one. I was under the influence of painkillers, but I believe I would have become just as enraged as I was about to even if I were not.

"You've got to be kidding!" I shouted. "You come in here at the last minute, spit out basic facts about three different types of blood thinners, and then expect me to make a decision like it's no big deal?!" I recall blasting.

The little I had gotten out of the information he'd relayed is that blood thinners, though necessary in my condition, can cause hemorrhaging. They all carry that risk, to different degrees, some with antidotes, and others, without. The side effects (which were alluded to but not fully explained) can be daunting. I knew a hasty decision may not be the best route to take, but without a lot of options, I made one in my compromised state and left.

I arrived home the evening of September 5. We finally had our entire family, along with our newest addition, gathered under the same roof. Becky and I were so thankful to have our family together, with everybody out of the hospital. The whole ordeal had been so fast-paced, we'd never had time to think much while it was going on. I'd had to react and make decisions and that's exactly what I had done.

The next day, my leg swelled up even bigger than before. The inside of my lower leg, just above my left ankle, felt like it was on fire. The ER was the last place in the world I wanted to go but we had no alternative.

Here I was again, being asked to tell my story multiple times to multiple people. It was determined that I'd been released too soon, before my platelets and red blood cell count had returned to a therapeutic level, and they'd started deteriorating. I remained in the hospital a total of eight days—long enough to get the swelling and pain under control and my blood work somewhat normalized.

Before I was discharged, Becky had to bring Jace back into the ER. She had our newborn in tow, suspecting Jace's turn of events might warrant an admission. He was admitted to pediatrics again. His neck was swelling up again and he was not doing well. I was able to go to his room and spend time with him each day.

Discharged again on September 9, I went straight home; retrieved clothes, toiletries, and a blow-up mattress; and went right back to the hospital to be with Jace, Becky, and JoJo. The doctors decided they wanted to get him back into the operating room—this time, to clean out all the puss from the infection and place another drain in his neck for a day or two so it could fully drain. The medical team found there wasn't much fluid to evacuate, as what was once fluid was now hardened. They couldn't do anything. Jace was discharged again with oral antibiotics and a plan to have an MRI in two weeks. Two weeks after that would be sclerosis treatments.

On Thursday, September 18, Jace's neck was giving him all kinds of trouble. He was in a lot of pain, and his breathing, shallow. That was enough for me, except I was done messing around with the base hospital. I decided that we were going to drive to Seattle Children's Hospital. So once again, Becky, JoJo, Jace, and I took a trip to Seattle.

Seattle Children's Hospital delivered exceptional care. I wish I'd taken Jace there from day one. They're a children's specialty hospital, number one in the Northwest and one of the best in the country. The nurse that put Jace's IV in managed to do it the first time while he was asleep, without waking him. They took blood for labs and still did not wake him up. Becky started crying.

"I can't believe what all he had to go through on base, and then they do this . . . and while he is asleep!"

I hugged her and told her it was not her fault. We had made the best decision we could have under the circumstances. I explained that we should just be thankful to be there at that time so we could finally get our son the right treatment.

The hospital team was able to get the swelling and pain back under control, and outlined a very different plan for how they wanted to go about things. I talked to the attending surgeon from the otolaryngology department. He told me he did not like sclerosis treatments for Jace, and that Jace was a prime candidate for them to go in surgically to remove the problem. We all hoped that would be the end of it. The pediatric lymphatic-malformation specialist there told me he had performed many of these procedures before. It would take about three hours and they would keep him for two nights for observation. The doctor made us feel good about the direction in which we were headed. We scheduled Jace's surgery for about four weeks out: October 15. This would provide adequate recovery time from what he was currently going through. We loved Seattle Children's Hospital.

* * * *

In the days and weeks leading up to Jace's surgery, JoJo suffered several life-threatening events in which his airway became clogged. The first occurred on a highway when I was not present, and the police intervened to save his life. Repeated incidents occurred at home. Because I'd been trained by some of the best Special Forces medics my regiment had to offer, I was able to work on him, though his size and the inherent fragility of infants presented a challenge. This was followed by base hospital visits that included a thrice-failed spinal tap—essentially, a training exercise using my son as the dummy—and a loud conversation among ER medical personnel about what they could have done differently. As with the failed administration of the IV needle for JoJo's older brother, Jace, in which an NICU employee was finally called in to do it, they concluded pediatrics should have performed the spinal tap in the first place. Becky's Facebook post read:

Joe Adam is doing great. But he did have two episodes of acid reflux, they think to the point he stopped breathing. We were admitted to Madigan Army Hospital once again. He is still not back to his birth weight either. They are testing to make sure he doesn't have an infection anywhere.

Jace's surgery at Seattle Children's Hospital went well. My family and I survived our hospital ordeals. We have healthy children and, as a family, we came out of all that stronger than ever, though we were still dealing with my TBI. During those indescribably challenging six weeks, and without losing sight of the fact that I was nothing short of losing my mind from the neurological effects of the TBIs and the drinking, somehow something turned over in me. The pressure I was under triggered a stress response I'd only previously felt in combat. I was baffled by how I was able to make decisions and chart multiple courses of action while in my state and circumstances at that time. I was able to pull myself up and latch onto the crisis-management skills outlined in my **SoP**— the predetermined ones I'd written to draw upon in those moments of life and death. Using them as a foundation, I was able navigate and make decisions. Despite being on a multitude of meds, drinking, and having one son born while the other was on the operating table, I was able to default to my foundational level of training: Complete the mission and get everybody back home safely. Now it was going to be up to me to get myself to a different kind of safety.

CHAPTER 4

The Power to Choose

When I was injured, I lost perspective. Fighting for my life as I knew it, I'd gotten myself into a state in which I'd begun to feel sorry for myself; it had become my frame of reference. Instead of the optimism that had been with me for as far back as I could remember, and which had propelled me through every eventuality I could think of, I now operated from a very dark place. It was akin to some kind of negative-energy field that followed me everywhere. I began to refer to it as "The Darkness." It lived in my room. It took on a life of its own.

Told by the military I could not sustain another blow to the head, I could no longer answer my calling. I would not be going back into combat. My former life as a Special Forces operator was entirely out of reach. I had no end state, no meaning, no goals, no purpose. I was aimless. There was no significance to my existence. Thoughts that my family would be better off without a drunken demon living among them 24/7 raced through what was left of my short-circuiting brain.

I associated The Darkness with the blast that had briefly knocked me out, back in Wardak, when it was all so black that I'd thought it was nighttime. I'd temporarily lost the sun to the dust and debris from the blast. Only now, it felt like eternal night. It never cleared up. I would languish in the idea that I was going to be mentally and emotionally disabled, unable to do the things I thought I was supposed to do or was truly meant to do.

NICoE had succeeded on some levels and failed on others—perhaps fundamentally. I went in on four to six drugs, largely controlled substances. After the blood clots, my total increased to thirteen, including antipsychotic drugs, sedatives, sleeping pills, and more. These included Zoloft, Wellbutrin, Zonegran, Adderall, Ambien, Percocet, Dilaudid, and Maxalt. But it wasn't going to work for me to spend my life strung out; I had to find a way to get past that. I began to understand that the steps toward my end state—my ultimate goal—involved first getting better for my family, and then for others I may be able to help. I had run this incredible gauntlet of fear and frustration, but it was now behind me—more in perspective. I was going to use it as a springboard to find my way.

* * * *

Jace left Seattle Children's Hospital with an all-clear, JoJo was out of the woods, and my blood clot appeared to be under control for the time being. No matter what had happened in the past, it was time to take ownership of my life. I wanted it back.

I remember being at Jace's bedside in the hospital. I had looked at my son and told myself that this was going to go one of two ways. I could continue to blame the course conventional medicine had laid out for me—a steep, jagged path I climbed each day with a tub of alcohol, and eventually carrying a backpack of thirteen mind-altering narcotics and other heavy meds, which was setting me up for death and the destruction of my family. Or I could embrace my pain—channel it correctly—and act on it to improve my situation.

From that moment on, I chose the latter. I made an immutable decision not to give external objects and obstacles power over me. I called upon a newfound focus to change what I didn't like about my current condition: everything. From that point on, I understood the power of choice—that I had it in me to decide how I would receive, process, and respond to external circumstances in my life. It was an epiphany. The shackles were gone. I was back on the battlefield—where I'd felt the most comfortable, confident, and in control—but this time, instead of committing to die, I was committing to live. It was time to put one foot in front of the other and walk out. I was done. **D**elta. **O**scar. **N**ovember. **E**cho. But, in effect, my journey was just beginning

The epiphany I had at my son's hospital bed led me to a point where I understood I needed a reconceived sense of meaning, goals, and purpose to survive what was happening to me. That's when clarity set in. I knew I had to establish what these now were. At that time, it also became clear that there were elements I'd put in place from my former life that I could grab onto. In my **Standard of Performance,** my personal code of ethics, I'd noted that in matters of life and death there isn't time to create a game plan. It has to be in place, as mine was, and for me at that point, it was clearly a matter of life and death. I did not want to live out the remainder of my existence in the ranks of the walking dead. I revisited my **Standard of Performance**. To begin with:

"If you can meet with Triumph and Disaster
And treat those two imposters just the same . . ."
—Rudyard Kipling, "If"

The real measure of life is how the race is run. Triumph and disaster are only by-products. To run the best race, one must cultivate a process in which a laser-sharp focus results in the capacity to plan, prepare, and perform to the best of one's abilities.

British philosopher and author James Allen wrote, "A man is literally what he thinks, his *character* being the *complete sum of all* his thoughts." Whether you believe that you can or that you can't, you're right. You cannot control what happens to you in life, but you can control what you will feel and do about what happens, and so, in one way or another, you can shape your circumstances.

So there it was: the blueprint. I was no longer an athlete. I was no longer a Special Forces operator. But I was a husband, father, brother, son, and human being. I had the same potential I'd always had, only now I was tasked with reinventing it. I had to determine my purpose and the "why" behind it.

* * * *

My newfound purpose, my "why," was to be the man that my wife and five children needed me to be, and I knew I couldn't do so on all the medication I was taking. The "how" remained to be seen, but if you have a big enough "why" you can always figure out the "how." My plan was to regain optimal health to be the man my family so desperately needed. Everything was a challenge in my condition, and I recalled what my father had said to me during one of my lowest moments.

"You know, Son, I can't begin to understand everything that you've been through, and I know you're hurting, but if you can find a way to make your mission about somebody else, and work on helping others, then I think you'll find that will be able to help you."

He had been right, though at that moment, I hadn't been entirely open to what he was saying. There had been too much going on and I couldn't hear it. Later, I would come to understand and really embrace the concept, focusing on other brain-injured members of the military for whom status-quo military remedies and solutions had not worked. In fact, by virtue of their failure, these "solutions" had often made the condition worse. Keeping all this in mind would make up my end state. And despite my impairments, I had to make a plan to get there.

* * * *

I had been fed a lot of misinformation. I don't believe any of it was intentional; misinformed, unengaged people give out misinformation. No matter how educated or ranked they are, it's bound to happen. I was consistently told that symptoms from a TBI do not appear weeks and months after a brain injury. If they're going to occur, they occur then and there—maybe in the days that follow, but not four, five, or six months later as mine did. That thinking is not accurate. My injuries developed later and intensified over time. My biochemical imbalances became more extreme and chaotic as hormones continued to leach, unchecked and untreated, from my brain. I suffered from low energy and libido, depression, anger and all-out rage, double vision, balance problems, cognitive issues, uncontrolled emotional outbursts, panic attacks, and more—the fallout from brain inflammation and leaking hormones. I had gone from being a Special Forces operator in possession of the highest performance standards a human being can achieve, to someone who could barely make it through the day.

Because I didn't have much going on inside, I had to be resourceful on the outside. I keep bringing up my **Standard of Performance**, and that's because it was and continues to be a life raft. It's where my course of action in dire circumstances had been scripted years before. Naturally, I was angry, but anger in the right context is a very powerful emotion—a useful tool—not something from which one should necessarily run. Earlier in my life, I'd made some emotional decisions from a place of anger, but they were unconstructive and did not forward the action. But later, having a "why": my family and others with similar injuries, and my **Standard of Performance** proved to be a profound catalyst for change.

* * * *

The Internet was the first place I visited in this new phase. I found a woman named Debbie Lee, a.k.a. "Momma Lee," whose son, Marc, was the first Navy SEAL killed in Operation Iraqi Freedom, at Ramadi. Debbie Lee founded AmericasMightyWarriors.org. Through her, I learned about hyperbaric oxygen therapy (HBOT) for TBIs. Because the treatment was considered unconventional, I'd have to go outside the military system, and so I asked Debbie Lee for some direction on this. I could see the road ahead would be a challenge, but when I was operational, I used to say, "We're going to take the hard right instead of the easy left." In other words, *We're going to do the right thing regardless of whether or not it's an inconvenience. If we have to get off the beaten path, fine, but we're going to get there.* And I was going to get better.

Most of life is out of our control, but not all of it. Being buried by circumstances is one thing, but realizing that there are choices, no matter how limited they may seem at the outset, is the first step in walking out and getting on track. Being able to flick that switch from off to on again, marshaling all my internal forces as I did in Wardak when I came to from the blast, was profound. I remember the exhilaration I felt at the time I came to understand that I could apply this to most anything. It was my ticket out. It can be anyone's ticket out, no matter what their circumstances.

So now I had my plan and a manageable task en route to my end state. I thought the HBOT might be the answer, but my command would not fund it. I knew I'd have to go outside the military system, though at the time, I didn't understand just how much economics would factor into my quest to get my life back. I had been hoping to find something in Washington State, where I was living, but there were no HBOT facilities close by. Debbie Lee also advocated other seemingly successful therapies, including those practiced at one of the nation's preeminent brain-rehabilitation centers: Carrick Brain Centers (now Cerebrum Health Centers). She used her influence to get me accepted into the two-week program as quickly as possible. Once again, my command refused to pay for it, stating I'd have to go on leave and fund it myself. It was during the time Jace was hospitalized at Seattle Children's Hospital, but he was on the other side of his surgery and recuperating well. Becky was so accomplished at taking the reins while I was deployed, and again now, when I was ill, that there was no question I would go immediately.

CHAPTER 5

Moving Outside of the Box

With NICoE now squarely in the rearview mirror, my family assumed I'd been treated by the best. We wanted to believe it and had no reason not to do so. Why wouldn't it have been true? Surely everything was OK, but the dam continued to burst. The holistic, supportive, unified medical team at NICoE that had orchestrated my care was certainly very helpful, and much more than I'd had in the past. But I was still sick. Despite that, however, I was now able to return myself to the incentives—or the "whys," which were my family and the desire to eliminate the struggle for others who may be in the same position. I could keep myself going if I thought about that, though the growing sense of frustration and despair those closest to me experienced was overwhelming for all of us. I was still unwell—still caught up in the psychological darkness that continued to consume me—but not so buried, as I was before, that I could not see what my family was going through. We were all hurting. I was still trying to find a way out—a portal back into the life I'd once known.

My family was solidly behind my trip to Carrick, though the military was not. They were underwriting nothing. TRICARE, which is military insurance, didn't cover anything considered to veer from the course—such as Carrick—even though each course in the military-insurance playbook on brain-injury treatment had seemed to lead to a dead end.

As a by-product of the narcotics, antidepressants, and psychotics I was on, my symptoms and emotions were either temporarily masked (later to return) or amplified. My alcohol abuse—still far from under control—exacerbated the effects of the medications. I drank from the time I awoke to the time I went to bed. My head was all over the place.

I'll never forget taking a memory test while at NICoE. The person administering the test informed me that there was a piece of paper with seven different shapes on it.

"When I reveal the paper with the shapes on it, you'll have ten seconds to review it. The sheet will be collected when the time is up. Your job is to tell me what shapes you remember from the paper you just examined," he'd said. Pretty straightforward.

The paper was flipped over and I examined the seven shapes for ten seconds. I distinctly remember naming the first shape, a triangle. I did not recall any shapes after the first one. I was horrified. We repeated the test multiple times, all with the same result. I went back to my room and cried. I couldn't process and recall simple shapes in a safe, nonthreatening environment. I'd been having a lot of trouble with my short-term memory but this was the first time I was forced to acknowledge the deficit. The doctors at NICoE recommended I carry a pad and pen with me to write everything down because I would forget something I had heard or read just minutes earlier.

Later, at a funeral in Tampa, which my extended family attended, my brothers—unaware of my extreme forgetfulness—ridiculed me about my lack of recall. We'd interacted that way since we were kids (a kind of mental roughhousing we'd all enjoyed), but they had not understood at that point that I was not "fixed" and, in fact, in many ways, was getting worse. Sometimes I found myself asking even more questions about my condition than I'd done when I'd visited NICoE.

But now, through Debbie Lee, I had found Carrick, filled out a leave form (the only way I could get two weeks off to find answers for my condition was to categorize it as vacation time), and was on my way to Dallas.

The fact is, not only did I lack funds for the program, I also didn't even have transportation costs covered at that point. A nonprofit I contacted helped with airfare, and Carrick covered the cost of treatment. I was able to stay with my parents about twenty miles from Carrick's offices.

At Carrick, the emphasis was on functional neurology. Eye movements, including the way the eyes bounce, provided a glimpse into the workings of the brain. Gait and balance were measured, as were heart rate and blood pressure in different positions. Biofeedback and neurofeedback were high on their agenda: figuring out what parts of the brain are or are not communicating with other parts of the body. For example, the right parietal lobe is responsible for the left side of the body—for pushing blood flow to the left-side extremities. My stay at Carrick took place just a few weeks after the DVT, or blood-clot episode in my left leg, which the Carrick team suggested may have been caused by an improperly functioning right parietal lobe. Apparently, the lobe didn't recognize my lower left leg and foot as real estate. While at Carrick, my left foot was bluish in color while the right one was normal-looking, so it wasn't a huge step for them to figure it out. It's just that up until then, no one had ever tried. It had never come up.

It was also discovered I'd go from a lying and sitting heart rate of sixty-plus beats per minute to a standing heart rate of two hundred beats per minute. I learned that it was damage to my brain stem that caused the variance. At the time, they didn't want to overload me with projected information and more concern, but eventually, I learned that had I continued at that rate, it would have caused a massive stroke. However, we were able to change that course.

At NICoE, as well as at Carrick, I'd learned that in engaging in certain eye and hand-eye–coordination movements, as in forced repetition, neuropathways that had been destroyed by TBIs could be rebuilt. It's called "neuroplasticity." Reconnections or new connections can be formed, which, when I was able to accomplish it, improved the blood flow to my left leg and foot, presumably precluding future clots. Neuroplasticity was also instrumental in helping me get my heart rate back to a safe range under all circumstances. The exercises consisted of hours and hours of painstaking repetition: the eye movement practices, lying down to sitting up, sitting to standing, tilting by five degrees a table on which I was positioned, letting my body absorb and readjust. It was strenuous and tedious, but I was committed. I kept returning my focus to my family; it was part of my "why." By the end of the two intensive weeks, I was doing a lot better. Much to my family's relief, on day two, the first full day of treatment, I'd started sleeping through the night for the first time in months.

At Carrick, I felt empowered because it was also the first time I was getting help outside the military. I felt liberated and uninhibited in speaking candidly about what was really going on with me. When it came to my excessive alcohol consumption, I could be up front about that too, confessing I drank from the moment I got up to the moment I closed my eyes at night.

I recall having a consult with Carrick's head neurologist and medical director about the damage my drinking was creating. What was said to me cut me to the core. I can't recall it verbatim but I've done my best to summarize the essence of his point.

"You're still on the battlefield and there are forces attempting to kill you. The next time you feel like you need a drink, ask yourself, *Is this more important than my wife and children?* Make up your mind right now. What's more important: your family or having another drink? If it's your family, then put the drinking behind you. At your current rate of consumption, it will kill you sooner than anything else. Choose to win the fight today and everyday hereafter."

Right then and there, I made the decision I would not consume another drink. That was in October 2014, and I've honored it. I was, and continue to be, grateful for the reckoning.

After Carrick, the migraines I'd been experiencing subsided. I'd had double vision and blurred vision, and that attenuated as well. I had clarity of thought for the first time in a year. Some improvements were not sustainable. The reasons—which were not yet apparent and are explored in depth in Chapter 6—involved the failure to identify and treat the primary underlying condition: inflammation of the brain. In order for *any* treatment to work sustainably, it needs to occur in a neuropermissive environment, meaning, one prepared to receive it. Trying to navigate life with a brain or body riddled with inflammation and coupled with hormonal deficiencies is similar to planting flowers in sand. Most plants will not grow or thrive in that environment. The brain and body are no different. They need the right environment to experience growth.

During the time I was at NICoE and Carrick, and throughout a later stint at the Brain Treatment Center, although there were goals that were met, overall my brain was not geared to receive treatment due to unchecked inflammation.

The second part of creating a neuropermissive environment is correcting hormonal imbalances and deficiencies caused by impact to the brain, which had also never been addressed. I had no idea about any of this while undergoing various protocols at that point.

When I left Carrick, believing for a while I'd been healed, I decided to quit cold turkey the multitude of medications I'd been on since NICoE. While I'd been advised against doing it that way, I felt my life was beginning all over again and I was eager to jump in with both feet. The clarity of thought available to me was like a rush, and I didn't want to delay anything. My reasoning was that while the thoughts and emotions I was going to have to deal with (which occur when substances like drugs and alcohol are taken away) might be unpleasant, at least they'd be genuine. They'd be mine. They would not be there in the form of detritus from some mind-bending chemical. Once again, the "why" came up for me: I wanted to get back to my family mentally and emotionally as fast as I could. It's what drove me. I wanted to be present for them.

I recall talking with one of my best friends, the one after whom my son JoJo is named. I was lamenting about how awful I felt every day and how many drugs I was on. In another moment of reckoning, another wake-up call, Joe asked me to think about living instead of complaining.

"Why don't you stop taking things like Dilaudid, and see what life is like without them?" he asked pointedly. "Wise up. Quit complaining. Do something."

So my "whys" increased. I wanted to be there for my family; I wanted to be an example— and, I hope—a touchstone for others in similar conditions.

Getting off all the medications at once, and having stopped drinking altogether, was challenging. I wouldn't recommend it for most people, if anybody. But it was the course I chose. The time between that November and February was a very difficult period for me. I didn't have an extraordinary team of like-minded individuals to rely on anymore; I was alone. I remember thinking that this must be similar to the feeling we have before we die; no one can take our place or do it for us. The journey needs to be made alone.

Without consistently returning to the "whys" in my life, I would have lost my footing. I'd learned many lessons by that point, summarily that awareness when things aren't going in a productive direction is a crucial element of change. I'd set myself on a course and determined parameters that would propel the action as quickly as possible to give my family some kind of normalcy again.

They needed to feel loved and safe—to live their lives without the fear and apprehension of a father spinning out of control. I was working as hard as I could to achieve my goal with the tools I had, though limited, given my mental state.

* * * *

The next rung on the healing ladder for me was the Brain Treatment Center. Located in Newport Beach, California, and an affiliate of the USC Center for Neurorestoration, the BTC is billed as an interdisciplinary clinic with a deep focus on brain health and neuroscience.

I had met another Special Forces operator in a different location, who'd come to many of the same conclusions I had about brain health and the way we were dealing with it. He informed me about the BTC. Under the auspices of a pilot study, where Green Berets would receive treatment at no cost, I helped get a couple of soldiers out there, although the timing wasn't good for me at first. The fact is, the feedback had been mixed to begin with—some saying positive things, and others, that they'd experienced no change.

But just hearing that it had worked for even one other individual was enough for me to embark upon further investigation. I eventually took a four-day trip to Southern California, having taken out some extra credit cards to offset any out-of-pocket costs. On the Monday I arrived, I knocked on the front door, introduced myself, and explained that I'd sent other servicemen to them and now needed treatment myself. I met with the medical director and was accepted right away.

The results of an EEG showed my entire brain was basically one big theta wave, which means that, for all intents and purposes, it was asleep. I was told that my brain state was similar to that of someone with autism. Additional testing revealed that in addition to the sleep mode, parts of my brain were in hyperactivity, or flight mode. When you have these kinds of inconsistencies in the brain, they cause the behavioral symptoms I'd been having all along, including depression, anxiety, panic attacks, and more. If you think about the brain as broadcasting frequencies like a single radio station, but instead of receiving one frequency and pushing another out, it's receiving multiple frequencies on one station at the same time and trying to push them out, you're left with a jumble: a lot of static. Nothing will be understood clearly. With BTC technology and the assessment, I was asked to remain there for one month of complimentary treatment, which was impossible for me at the time because of other responsibilities at home. So I agreed to come back as soon as I could.

Back on base, with my trips to NICoE, Carrick, and the Brain Treatment Center, and an impending return trip to the BTC, I was beginning to be perceived as somebody who was difficult to deal with. When I spoke, people listened; that much hadn't changed. However, I could see a burgeoning agitation, as though I were trying to take advantage of the system. It couldn't have been further from the truth. Challenging the status quo is often met with resistance.

Going from being one of the most respected, proven, professional members of my unit to being seen as a nuisance and a burden who created more work for people was difficult for me to understand. But again, my "whys" allowed me to stay on point. I also saw others treated miserably. I realized that as bad as it was for me with my command, treatment was mitigated to some extent because of my status—the respect I'd earned prior to all this. But others weren't getting that. A twenty-year-old with a TBI didn't have a prayer in the current military medical system. I remember telling myself I was going to get better—completely better—no matter what the military thought of me. And I was going to make sure others got their lives back too. Those who were judging me and dictating to me had no idea about the difficult terrain those of us with TBIs were trying to navigate. Someone had to shine that light.

CHAPTER 6

The Underlying Condition

During a traumatic brain injury, the brain is jarred inside the cerebral spinal fluid. Neurons, the vessels that carry crucial chemicals from one place to another, are intended to house and transport these chemicals. When a TBI is sustained, neurons are sheared and the chemicals leak, causing neurotoxicity that results in oxidative stress/post-traumatic brain inflammation.

Returning the brain to a neuropermissive state, initially referenced in the previous chapter, requires getting rid of inflammation first and foremost, and addressing extreme hormonal issues created by the injury as well. For example, the pituitary gland, located at the base of the brain and regulated by the hypothalamus, houses nine hormones produced and secreted in the brain. When physical damage to the pituitary occurs, we lose one, two, three, or maybe all of those hormones, partially or entirely. So when there is brain swelling compounded by problems with the regulatory mechanism controlling hormones, it's a breeding ground for disaster. Before I met Dr. Gordon, none of this had been considered in my case.

At that point, I felt as though I'd been through every step-two program I could have. Step-two programs should only be offered after addressing the underlying condition, not before. All of them were supported by scientific data and leading experts in their fields, and all had merit and value. But without addressing the heart of the issue, the neuropermissive environment, those treatment modalities could not reach their full potential. They were doomed to fail.

In December of 2014, about a month after Carrick, I was interviewed by Fox News to help promote Carrick's work. At the time, the positive effects of my treatment were still active, although, unfortunately, subsiding. But when they asked, I wanted to help, as they'd done more for me than anyone at that point.

The wide exposure, unbeknownst to me and seen while I underwent the additional treatment at the Brain Treatment Center, resulted in my unit launching an investigation. It's called Army Regulation 15-6, where issues of "misconduct" that betray the uniform code of military justice are investigated. Facts and findings are sought, with investigators providing recommendations to higher-ups on a course of action. The protocol involves Judge Advocates, whose title, JAG, was made popular by the TV series of the same name. As we'd started our Warrior Angels Foundation during this time to help others with TBIs, the Army decided to determine if this was an abuse of my position as a Special Forces operator.

Though I'd been sure never to name names or even identify my unit in any way, my current battalion commander told me that my actions were unethical. My intent with the media had been to use their forums to highlight alternative therapies to those who might otherwise not have known about them. I believed my actions were altruistic and honorable. I was incredulous that my morals and ethics were being called into question. I'd made a concerted effort to neither implicate anyone in the mistreatment I'd received by the military on this quest to become whole again, nor overtly discredit the military health system. Sure, it had severe limitations, but I was careful in the way I expressed things. I still am. My reason for starting the Foundation was to provide help and resources for men and women, as injured and ill as I was—nothing more. It was a good cause, and still I was the subject of an investigation. Though not criminal in nature, more often than not, punitive actions or something other than an honorable discharge can result from this kind of thing, and it was a possibility.

The positive side of the Fox interview led Dr. Mark L. Gordon to us. A leader in the field of treating TBIs since 2004, Dr. Gordon viewed the Fox interview and contacted Adam and me directly. A TBI survivor himself, he told us he had very specific protocols he'd developed over the course of fourteen years and wondered if I would be interested.

He referred us to a podcast in which we watched him discuss the details of traumatic brain injury, the need to properly assess it through an objective blood panel, and how his protocol has effectively treated it. The podcast—hosted by comedian Joe Rogan (the *Joe Rogan Experience* #574)—featured Jason Hall, screenwriter of *American Sniper*, as well as former Navy Corpsman Matthew Gosney, who in many ways was rendered nonfunctioning following his own TBI. The military's attempt to handle his injury had included loading him up on narcotics, antidepressants, and other heavy drugs, as well as hospitalizing him for a suicide attempt that was eventually—through Dr. Gordon—connected to his TBI.

In World War II, the term for TBI was "shell shock," with Vietnam using its own label, but it's the same injury that has caused trauma to the brain and consciousness since the beginning. As long as there have been wars and sports, there have been TBIs. This was the first time I'd heard about service members and veterans being massively misdiagnosed as having post-traumatic stress disorder, when in fact, TBIs were the root cause. It felt as though I were hearing my own story all over again.

Through Dr. Gordon's twenty-eight-point hormone assessment, brain regulation of hormones is able to be assessed. The test isolates hormones to determine insufficiencies and deficiencies. Among other things, Matt was found to have low testosterone, as did I (something determined around the time JoJo was born, although never linked to my TBI). Deficient or insufficient levels of free testosterone is a prominent byproduct of a TBI. According to Dr. Gordon, most people think of hormones as gender- or sex-related, but in fact, testosterone is connected with inflammatory chemistry and repair of the body. When there is a deficit of testosterone, we pay a steep price, as both

Matt and I did. It cost us just about everything: our minds, our families, and our lives as we knew them.

* * * *

In early February 2015, Dr. Gordon and I sat down together for the first time as he ran a blood panel for the hormone assessment. The results wouldn't arrive for a few weeks, but I got to spend all morning with him. We were talking conversing so that he could obtain a baseline understanding of who I was and what my past experiences were, and learn about my painful navigation of the military healthcare system. Around lunchtime, I was given what's called a provocative testosterone injection, intended to determine how someone responds to testosterone. It's a normal dose that would be given to anyone, with the stipulation that the recipient charts his or her responses—how he or she is feeling—over the following sixty hours.

It was an incredible turnaround for me. I received the injection, and soon after, returned to my car for the drive back to Carlsbad, where I was staying at the time—about a two-hour trip from Dr. Gordon's office. Anyone who knows California also knows that the 405 Freeway is bumper-to-bumper, even under the best of conditions. This took place during another period of months (especially coming off the narcotics and other drugs, and withdrawing from the alcohol) in which I was having a lot of problems with anger, and anger turning to rage. It was an uncomfortable time, once again, for anyone around me.

I was alone on the return trip from Dr. Gordon's office when I found myself stuck in stop-and-go traffic, which typically would have sent me through the roof. I suddenly realized that nothing was bothering me. The knot, like a twisted fist that had taken up residence between my belly button and my rib cage for about a year and a half—otherwise known to me as "The Darkness," was gone. I was without anxiety. I recall thinking that I felt the way people do when the dental assistant takes that lead bib off your body just after an X-ray. I could draw a deep breath again.

The next thing I did was call Becky. We spent an hour talking about absolutely nothing. I had often struggled with what I'd considered trivial conversation—small talk—or even important conversations that took more than a couple of minutes. Sadly, I don't think I'd given Becky a chance for an in-depth conversation about *anything* in well over a year, let alone a normal one. She kept remarking during that drive that our talk was incredible. I felt this ray of hope that if this was what it was like to feel right again, I could achieve it. In those hours after the injection, I was without behavioral issues, including rage, depression, and anxiety—anything that had darkened my days for a long, long time. In a word, it was magnificent! I had returned to life, although I'd almost forgotten what life was.

At the sixtieth hour, right on the mark, I could actually feel the sensation of peace and calmness waning. The testosterone had run its course. I experienced the other symptoms rearing their ugly heads; I mean, I could tangibly feel them, like a possession in some horror movie. It was an indescribably difficult time because I wanted to hold onto what I'd been missing for so long— what I'd had over the past few days. Dr. Gordon explained that we needed to wait for the results of the blood panel to come back before administering anything else, or more of the same. Waiting for the results and just to feel good again was challenging. I felt like an addict craving my next fix. Simply feeling normal and operating from a level place was like an addict's high for me because I'd pretty much forgotten what it was like.

When the results came back, I was deficient in just about everything, just as Dr. Gordon had posited. I was without adequate testosterone, IGF-1, growth hormone, DHEA, you name it. My neurons had sheared and integral chemicals were leaking everywhere—all of this, a direct result of head trauma. The pituitary gland, controlled by the hypothalamus and the regulatory mechanism for all those hormones, had been damaged.

When I started on the right protocol, relief was rapid. It was an immediate transformation, just as I'd experienced in that two-hour drive down the 405 in Southern California. The fact is, the longer I am on the protocol, the more improvements I see as my brain consistently repairs itself, making its way back to where it was before my injuries.

So many things are not within our control, but some are. A Special Forces buddy of mine also had a TBI; actually, he'd been shot in the head on our last trip. Although for all intents and purposes, he "recovered," all kinds of behavioral problems resulted from the brain injury, including his receiving a DWI. The command couldn't understand why this guy couldn't show up on time and was so forgetful. He was put in a twenty-eight-day inpatient detox program in Oregon and I drove up to visit him. I found him totally consumed by rage and hate. He was right to feel that way, however, as his medical condition had been mishandled and he'd been mistreated to the highest degree. I tried to explain to him that I'd learned these terrible lessons myself, though those who are tasked with getting us to our recovery, while misguided, are not necessarily trying to put one over on us. They don't set out each morning to destroy us; it's just that they are uninformed or, in some cases, don't care.

Later, I reminded myself of the day in the not-too-distant past when I'd decided how I wanted all this to go. I continue to tell people, "If you want to get better, work on what you *can* control. Don't dwell on what you can't." I can't guarantee an outcome to anything in my life, but I can guarantee my attitude and the effort I make. I have control over those things. Stop focusing on what's going wrong and what's out of your control. If it's out of your control, then what can be done about it? Your focus may be clogging you up because it's channeled into negativity. Redirect it to having the best attitude and most powerful effort you can possibly make. Let go of the hold hate has over you. Give it no dominion. Once I had made that decision, I was free to begin to take back my life.

CHAPTER 7

Abundance

Along the way, in an effort to ease the financial burden my family incurred in light of my ongoing medical issues, my research revealed that in some states, Purple Heart recipients get a property tax exemption. Texas, where we were now living, was one. Further research showed that because of my military record and the injuries I'd incurred in my years of service, I met all the requirements several times over. Nobody in my command had thought to put in for one, so a year after I returned, I brought it to their attention. They readily agreed.

Purple Heart applications go through a long bureaucratic process, beginning with about a half-dozen supervisors—right on up the chain.

Sometimes paperwork gets mired in the mix and lost, and mine got lost more than once, needing to be reissued several times over the course of a year. Ultimately, the Purple Heart was denied with the explanation that I'd initiated the explosive charges on that mission in Wardak that had briefly knocked me out. On that basis, my injuries (so severe, they'd resulted in medical retirement) and exemplary military record apparently didn't warrant a Purple Heart.

Another surprise came in the form of TSGLI denial. Traumatic Injury Protection is a rider to SGLI, or Servicemember's Group Life Insurance. According to eligibility requirements, it is automatically provided as short-term financial assistance to severely injured service members and veterans to assist in recovery. By way of further explanation, TSGLI is not only for combat injuries, but also provides insurance coverage for injuries incurred on and off duty.[4] In short, as I did in my application for the Purple Heart, it appeared from an evidentiary perspective that I qualified for this entitlement several times over. Upon TSGLI denial because of "insufficient evidence," we appealed—twice, in fact—noting each time that the notification process following an appeal takes more than one hundred business days because they are so backlogged. The package

4 http://www.benefits.va.gov/insurance/tsgli.asp

we'd put together was meticulously structured, detailed, and accurate, dissecting the injury, the myriad ways in which I was affected, and how it all related to the TSGLI prerequisites for the claim.

The third entitlement strikeout on my road to recovery was in the form of Social Security Disability Insurance. Again, I was seeking *earned* entitlements—nothing I didn't deserve, for which I wasn't qualified, or for which I had no business applying. I was made to understand that if I could no longer do my job in the Army and was on my way out via a medical evaluation board decision, I would be eligible for SSDI. It would come in handy during the months I was struggling through recovery but not yet receiving medical retirement benefits from the service—the time leading up to and including that ten-month gap. We applied. The claim, also diligently prepared with no shortcuts just like the TSGLI claim, was also twice denied for "insufficient evidence."

An attorney we hired for the third SSDI appeal was able to advance things to the point where the State of Texas, saying it had decided the psychological-testing process the VA uses is insufficient, ordered me to redo all of the neuropsychological tests that we'd already done. I told them, *no thanks.* I wasn't going to trade my time to redo something that was already well documented.

* * * *

When someone in the military is injured or sick, a medical evaluation board uses a process called a "profile," with a ratings system for the severity of the matter. If a soldier breaks a leg and is unable to participate in anything physical for six months, that individual will be ranked by a specific letter and number. At the end of that time, a reevaluation is undertaken in which the soldier will be allowed to return to active duty, or perhaps downgraded, or upgraded to a category not as severe.

With my TBI, which was considered a permanent injury and rated P3 ("P" for permanent)—as opposed to something potentially curable, such as a broken leg—the medical evaluation board is charged with determining if the injury is a disqualifying condition. In this realm, one may be disqualified from service within their specific occupational specialty. If reclassification is warranted, that individual may be medically retired and shifted to another job or duty, or retired from the Army altogether.

My mind-set for a very long time was that I wanted to get back to being operational, and I was going to do whatever was needed to ensure that happened. It may sound extreme, but if I could not get there by the proverbial book, I was willing to lie, cheat, or steal to return to my role as a Special

Forces Green Beret. In short, I wanted combat at any cost. It was my whole identity. Before the blood clot to my leg and lungs, I conjured the thought that it was possible to return to active duty, or at least I could pull all the right strings to propel myself back into an operational job somewhere within the regiment. I was dedicated. I was in demand. People wanted me on their team.

But after the blood clot, it became abundantly clear that I could not work my way out of where I was. The anticoagulants I was instructed to take for the rest of my life rendered me highly risky combat material, along with the possibility of clots reoccurring. Because of this, in November of 2014, I requested my command move ahead with the P3 profile process, which got formally underway the following month. As much as I grappled with my decision, the condition was black-and-white: I was out of commission. There was no reason to fight it and drag out the inevitable for months or years.

I'm not desk-job material. From my perspective, the last thing in the world a Special Forces operator wants is to spend forty hours a week in a chair, inside a cubicle, which was offered to me. But for me, it was all or nothing. No combat? No deal.

The medical-retirement review process involves military physicians, experts in their respective fields, reviewing every condition the petitioner has stated as a basis for medical retirement. Each condition must be ranked, with criteria used for levels of severity, disqualifying factors that may impede or prohibit performing current duties, and much more. It is highly detailed. I came out with thirty-two different issues or disabilities. Twenty-two were rated and they decided that the remaining ten had not been caused by my time in the service, which, of course, was inaccurate. I'd not had them before I served. The bottom line, however, was that of the twenty-two, I was ranked as 100 percent disabled according to the U.S. Department of Veterans Affairs. The two disqualifying conditions were the deep vein thrombosis (blood clot) and post-traumatic headaches—not the TBI itself! Interesting. Regardless, I would be retired.

I was still dealing with erratic behavioral issues at that point, not firing on all cylinders, and now I needed to cope with the loss of my identity as an active and respected Green Beret. Being sensitive to the emotional fallout that would ensue—rather than trying to avoid it—would be important in moving forward in my life. It's hard enough for someone whole to make a conscious decision to leave something they love. But when the decision has essentially been made for you because you now have limitations, it's hard to accept. So I had to be open to what I might feel as it unfolded.

Special Forces team members have a bond. At home or amid death and destruction, it's very much a locker room atmosphere. It has to be to stay positive and focused. The last time someone turns in their equipment, or kit, which is tied to all of these emotionally charged events in combat, it's a giving up of the life they know. It's like an athlete turning in a uniform. In war, we make sacrifices, and this was just a different kind of sacrifice. For me, Special Forces was what I'd done most of my adult life. It was overwhelmingly sad. I had to keep returning to my "whys," believing life could start over for my family and me. I was capable of that leap. I was free to invest my time in developing our Foundation.

Here's a Facebook post of mine from May 9, 2015: *I'm starting a newsletter about traumatic brain injuries and turning obstacles into opportunities. I'm putting the finishing touches on "How to Conquer a TBI: A Former Green Beret's Quest and His Challenge to You." Please e-mail me if you would like to receive it. I turned in my kit this week. I never would have guessed turning it in would have been such an emotional event, but it provided me much-needed closure. I'm starting this next chapter with this newsletter. Please share if you think someone would benefit from this.*

In retrospect, I'd made the decision to live a life worth living, both for me and for others like me. TBIs are an immense, widely misunderstood issue, both by conventional medicine and by its sufferers, along with their loved ones and friends.

Repurposing my life could result in repurposing other lives. I had to find the discipline to return myself to that concept every day. And I had to remember that even with my limited (pre-Dr. Gordon) cognitive function, it wasn't about my internal resources, but about how resourceful I could be. I believed and had confidence in my abilities. It was time to put them to work somewhere else.

With a 100 percent service-connected disability rating by the VA, one would assume compensation was imminent. Ditto for Army retirement compensation. I had to support my family and though I hadn't taken a salary from our new Foundation, I was trying to become flush enough to get it off the ground. These are monetary entitlements that I'm talking about, which are earned—not something undeserved or unearned.

Unfortunately, before your official separation date, the last paycheck for two weeks' worth of work is held in the process, and then the entitlements don't start for thirty to sixty days. My family and I went a couple of months without any income. My monthly Army retirement compensation didn't begin until ten months following my official retirement.

I'd covered any associated costs for treatment I received outside of the military including transportation, lodging, and food. I had also covered the cost for Becky to come out and stay with me during my last week at NICoE, which encourages the spouses to come for the last week. There are educational classes for them as well as opportunities to learn from different medical experts about TBI and how it affects their loved one. My command had told me that the unit would reimburse me for Becky's cost to visit me. At the time, Becky was seven months pregnant with JoJo and we had to fly my parents up from Texas to watch our girls in Washington State. I returned from NICoE and filed the travel voucher to recoup the reimbursement we had been promised. I was informed by command that upon a further review of policy, we would not be reimbursed.

I'd had unblemished credit prior to my injuries and no trouble getting a couple more credit cards to pay for all my health costs. The credit cards also allowed us to live for those ten months while waiting for our earned entitlements to come in. We sank further into debt the longer we waited. By the spring of 2016, we found ourselves buried in substantial debt and filed for Chapter 7 bankruptcy. Once my pay was turned on, we had enough to cover our needs, but there was nothing left over to go toward the debt.

Our focus is our most precious commodity. For Becky and me, wealth means having the freedom to use one's time and focus in the way one wishes to use it. I was free to invest all my time and focus on my family and the Warrior Angels Foundation. All our basic needs were met. I was living my purpose again. I considered going to work on an offshore oil rig, but for what? After I analyzed our current situation, the decision was easy. I am the master of my time, focus, and destiny. I'm not trading them to do something that doesn't align with my Standard of Performance.

Filing for bankruptcy is a highly stressful time for most. I remember the conversation I had with Becky after the process was over. We both agreed that we couldn't be any happier than we were at that moment. We were living a purposeful life full of love, growth, and contribution. Filing for bankruptcy didn't define or validate us, but the reasons and the decision to file surely did. We were living lives focused on family, and bringing resources and healing to one of the most wounded sectors of the military in a way no one else before us had done. We had wealth. We had unlimited abundance.

CHAPTER 8

Creating the Warrior Angels Foundation

The idea of starting a foundation to help our traumatic-brain-injured brothers and sisters seemed like a monumental a task when it first occurred to us—but we could not ignore it. The concept was something we'd never have considered as the journey unfolded, nor did we anticipate doing anything in the future—that is, until a pivotal moment at Carrick Brain Centers in 2014.

I recall thanking the program coordinator, wanting to give something back, and asking what I could do to help in some way. I had no idea what it could be. Though Carrick didn't turn out to be the final key to my recovery, at that juncture, it had done more for me than anything that had preceded it, and in a short amount of time. I wanted to pay it forward.

"Well, we certainly have the medical team in place," the coordinator informed me, "but we have a waiting list because we don't have the resources to get people here and treated."

A waiting list? There were those out there who were affected and suffering as badly, or maybe even worse, than I was, and they had to wait for treatment? At that moment, I felt as though I'd been struck by lightning. People use that expression loosely, but I really did. It was like a charge went through me that would further change how I operated in the world. From time to time, I'd go back in my mind to what my father had said about "making it about somebody else." This was one of those times.

With all that had happened to me, I was fortunate. Though I'd gone through things alone and in an impaired state, somehow I'd picked myself up, had begun to climb out, persevered, and found relatively unknown, alternative therapies in the face of an inordinate number of obstacles. These ranged from mental and physical impediments to people who put up roadblocks—on purpose or inadvertently—to my recovery. But we are all different: I knew that not everyone with a TBI could ultimately be tenacious in the way I'd been. That's where the idea for a foundation to help them get started began, and Adam and I began to investigate the complex world of nonprofits.

It may sound less than humble, but starting a foundation and making it fly is not for the faint of heart. Passion is a requisite, as is the determination to keep your cause front and center at all times. I felt a strong calling to help others—to lessen their pain. Hundreds of thousands of people hear that kind of calling, ending up in ministry, medicine, education, law, and other fields. This was mine. I knew that because of my background, credibility, and the fact that I had *lived* everything, I could speak from a powerful platform. I could be heard by those who really needed to hear me, helping those who really needed help. I never wanted to forget the strangers who'd gone out of their way to lift my family and me up, and though I didn't know what to do or how to do it, I could now create an opportunity to give it back.

In November and December of 2014, we started to research and organize in order to file our nonprofit paperwork. On January 5, 2015, we achieved 501(c)(3) status in the state of Texas. As nonprofits go, we started with nothing, or certainly very little, but with a goal of giving everything to the people who needed us.

From what I know, motivational powerhouse Tony Robbins, who has inspired me for a long time, also started that way. Years ago, he told the story of the genesis of his empire—which was built by being of service when he was totally broke, unemployed, living without furniture (and maybe even not enough food), and sitting in the middle of the floor of his four-hundred-square-foot apartment. As I understand it, Robbins's lightning-bolt moment came when he realized that he was all he had; he was his only commodity, making the point that if the glass were half full, he was *everything* (not just all). "All" sounds like scarcity. He'd decided he was substantial. He was enough, and he started from there. When it came to forming our foundation, I similarly asked myself, *Who am I? What am I bringing to this? Nobody else has had my life experiences. That's what I can bring. That's substantial. That's enough. That's* everything.

Though Adam officially "ETSed" (definition: expiration—term of service) from the Army in October 2015, he'd had enough leave saved up to be able to return to Texas a few months ahead of that to work full time in moving the Warrior Angels Foundation forward. He revamped our administrative and logistical systems to full compliance in facilitating the greatest number of people possible through the Foundation.

At first, though, without a lot of marketing and press to cast a wide net, we reached out to a network of people we knew from the military community who needed immediate help. We wanted to get to them with a variety of treatment options—the ones I'd experienced along the way. In June of 2015, we decided to channel funding exclusively to candidates for Dr. Gordon's protocols, which was what we wanted to endorse. The others had gotten me to a certain point, but his had given me my life back. He'd identified and worked to resolve the underlying conditions: inflammation, the dysregulation of hormones, neurosteroids— the big, enduring picture.

With Dr. Gordon, we have phenomenal results for a fraction of what the other treatment modalities cost. Additionally, through technology, no one has to be uprooted from his or her geographical location and leave his or her family. Patients can receive world-class care and results at home. It was clear we needed Dr. Gordon, and by virtue of the relationship, we wanted to support additional scientific research for him to take the protocols to the next level.

Fortunately, since its inception, the Warrior Angels Foundation has become well known and respected in the nonprofit world, where there are forty thousand veteran support organizations. We've been on major news networks, in national newspapers, part of countless podcasts, and in various other online forums.

Just as we'd hoped, as airtight as the protocol was long before Dr. Gordon began working with me, the Foundation has turned into a proving ground for it. Findings will soon be published in scientific journals, which, in turn, will broaden our visibility, viability, and outreach. A peer-reviewed process by an independent review board will validate everything, which will subsequently forward the action, so that we can bring in more TBI sufferers whose lives we hope to change.

* * * *

The fact is, in the broadest possible sense, we believe that what we're doing has a potential benefit for everyone. We're using the veteran population to highlight a problem that is identifiable on a much larger scale. Our end state is that we want Dr. Gordon's protocols to be implemented by the Veterans Administration and the Department of Defense. In this respect, national security will be strengthened. For a TBI sufferer, we can first establish a baseline, monitor the individual, and identify when somebody begins to have—or even has the potential for—the issues I experienced. However, for me (and others), they weren't apparent for weeks and months after the actual incident(s). We can prevent people from ever having to deal with the neuropsychological deficits that traumatic brain injury can cause.

By virtue of this practice, spouses and families will be strengthened and remain intact, rather than being threatened, buffeted, and torn apart by the fallout. We will be able to keep highly valued members of the armed forces in the ranks, firing on all cylinders, rather than losing skilled, meticulously trained and experienced operators who can no longer function. This bolsters national security.

The annual cost to the taxpayer for a veteran with traumatic brain injury and post-traumatic stress is about $15,000 a year. That money goes to psychotherapy and medication, often exacerbating the problem. Over the course of an injured individual's lifetime, that cost is only going to increase as his or her mental and physical health deteriorates.

Our costs through the Foundation are about one-third of that. Funds will go to treat the underlying conditions so people can get better and come off mind-altering narcotics and other medications that never address the core issues to begin with. Our biggest expenses are currently laboratory costs, which will lower as performance rises. When you look at the savings, it's dramatic. Why *wouldn't* the VA and DoD climb on board? There is no downside. The Warrior Angels Foundation is here to free the medically oppressed.

CHAPTER 9

Biology Lessons Learned Relative to TBI

Environment Trumps DNA

Bruce H. Lipton, PhD, is a former medical-school professor and research scientist. His book, *The Biology of Belief,* informs us that our cells are controlled by their environment, and not their DNA. Dr. Lipton was one of the first researchers to work with human stem cells back in the 1970s.

What he discovered has sparked a new science called "epigenetics." Dr. Lipton cloned identical stem cells, placed them in different culture mediums, and documented how the identical stem cells performed in the varied environments. When the environment was altered, the stem cells produced strikingly separate reactions. Stem cells in one environment produced muscle. When the environment was altered, identical stem cells produced bone. And when the environment was again altered, identical stem cells produced fat. All the stem cells were identical, and up until this point, it was commonly believed that our DNA was responsible for how cells grow and mature.

Dr. Lipton's work suggests that we are not preprogrammed automatons (victims of our DNA), destined to play out a life that has already been decided by our genetic makeup. Changing the environment in which stem cells are kept allows them to turn into things that were previously thought to be impossible. This has been scientifically proven down to the most basic cellular level. Our bodies are a community of about fifty to seventy trillion cells. Therefore, it is our beliefs, our own perceptions of how the world works, that directly influence our biology.

LESSONS LEARNED

Epigenetics is the study of changes in an organism caused by modification of genetic expression due to environmental factors, and not the alteration of the genetic code itself. It is our beliefs, not our genes, that shape our biology.

We are the creators of our world. What we think becomes our reality.

Hypothalamic-Pituitary-Adrenal (HPA) Axis

The hypothalamus is the portion of the brain that interprets perceptions of the outside world. The hypothalamus sends a chemical message based on its perceptions of the outside world to the pituitary gland. The anterior pituitary plays a central role in the production and release of chemical messengers into the bloodstream. The chemical messengers stimulated by the hypothalamus and produced by the pituitary gland are called "tropic hormones." Tropic hormones are released into circulation, arriving at target organs to release a physiological response. For example, the adrenal glands receive a chemical message from the pituitary gland, activating stress hormones to elicit the physiological response known as "fight or flight."

LESSONS LEARNED

Head trauma affects the HPA Axis. The hypothalamus is the portion of the brain that interprets perceptions of the outside world and then sends that information to the pituitary gland. The pituitary gland sends a message to the rest of our body to elicit a physical response. Science has revealed that our beliefs directly influence our biology, but damage to these areas of the brain can cause a shearing of the circuitry, leading to deficits of our cognition, behavior, and physiology.

Fight or Flight

The stress response from the adrenal glands equips the body with a physiological response that allows us to fight our way out of a hostile situation or to run until the threat no longer exists. This physiological response constricts blood flow from certain areas of the body in order to send increased blood flow to others. Blood is sent to our arms and legs to aid in the fight-or-flight response. The stress response also constricts blood vessels in the forebrain, while sending more blood to the hindbrain, the reflex center of the brain. Reflexive behavior due to a lack of blood flow to the forebrain dominates our conscious thoughts while we are under stress. This response is a restrictive response in which less intelligent reflexive behavior dominates how we interact with the immediate environment.

Humans have outpaced our evolutionary biology, but we're still running on the old operating system. Our stress responses have been a saving grace, allowing us to escape a tiger or empower a mother who needs to lift a car to get to her baby. As soon as the threat is neutralized or evaded, that response leaves our bodies, allowing us to grow and prosper.

Today, for the great majority of us, the fight-or-flight response is rarely, if ever, needed in our daily lives. The current pace of technological innovation has created a population that appears to be stressed out on a routine basis. Our perceptions of the world create stress responses in our bodies to fight or flee from things that do not exist in the physical world, because that's the story and the pattern being played on auto-loop in our minds. Our ancient operating system can't understand whether or not the threat caused by a stressor we've imagined (e.g., an overdue bill) is gone or still present. The constant bombardment of e-mails, texts, twenty-four-hour negative-news networks, social media, and worry over things over which we have no control are deleterious to our health.

LESSONS LEARNED

The stress response from the adrenal glands equips the body with a physiological response called "fight or flight." This response is a restrictive response in which less intelligent reflexive behavior dominates how we interact with our environment. Humans have outpaced our evolutionary biology, but we're still running on the old operating system. Our perceptions of the world create stress responses in our bodies to fight or run from things that do not exist in the physical world. The resulting chronic stress is debilitating to our health. The result of a non-neuropermissive environment from head trauma can stimulate a less intelligent reflexive response. This is precisely the reason why I lost it on that guy in the parking lot and couldn't understand why.

Neurons and Glial Cells

Neurons process and transmit information by way of electrical and chemical signals. Glial cells are non-neuronal cells that can inhibit or activate neurons, connect to neurons, or control the activity of neurons, in addition to providing support and protection to both the peripheral and central nervous system's neurons. The latest in neuroscience suggests that 10 percent of our brain cells are comprised of neuronal cells, with glial cells making up the other 90 percent.

Glial cells are essential and instrumental in the functional integration of how the brain works. Glial cells also produce neurosteroids in the brain. Dr. Bruce Lipton makes this analogy: "Think of neurons as the noun in a sentence, and the glial cells are the verbs, adjectives, adverbs, and the modifier to all the nouns." The proper functioning of our glial cells is integral to a healthy brain. Science has revealed that glial cells play a much bigger role than just supporting our neurons, as once believed.

Glial cells, which were previously thought to only play a supporting role to neurons, are instrumental in the functional integration of how the brain works. Head trauma from blast-wave exposure can lead to microtears of glial cell and neurons. The microtearing can result in a non-neuropermissive environment, leading to neuroinflammation and neurosteroid dysfunction.

Neurosteroids

Neurosteroids were first discovered in 1985. Until then, we did not know that hormones were both produced and synthesized in the brain by the glial cells. The following excerpt is from Dr. Mark L. Gordon's book *Traumatic Brain Injury: A Clinical Approach to Diagnosis and Treatment*:

> Whenever we speak in the terms of hormones, we are generally referring to those produced by the peripheral glands (neuroactive steroids) and not those made in the brain (neurosteroids).

> Neurosteroids play important functions in neurodevelopment and neuronal remodeling,

including neurogenesis, axonal and dendritic growth, and synaptic connectivity. In addition to their protective effects on the brain, neurosteroids can regulate myelin formation and increase expression of myelin proteins in the sciatic nerve.

It appears that neuroactive steroids are the macro-hormones of bodily function, while neurosteroids are the micro-hormones that fine-tune the interactions amongst the neuro-circuitry of the brain. Neurotransmitters and their corresponding receptors are responsible for inter-activity and reactivity of control and modulation systems within the brain. Failure of this system will lead to erratic transmissions, which are perceived as major patho-psychiatric events. Depression and suicide, anxiety and panic attacks, and phobias and psychoses are all representative of this condition of unpredictable effects of neurosteroid dysfunction.

LESSONS LEARNED

Neurosteroids are produced by the glial cells in the brain, while neuroactive steroids are produced by the peripheral glands. Neurosteroids play important functions in neurodevelopment and neuronal remodeling, including neurogenesis, axonal and dendritic growth, and synaptic connectivity. Head trauma can cause a failure of this system, leading to erratic transmissions, which can be perceived as depression and suicide, anxiety and panic attacks, and phobias and psychoses. These are all representative effects of neurosteroid dysfunction.

Traumatic Brain Injury

Traumatic Brain Injury is a two-phase injury. Phase I, the initial injury to the brain, can come by way of an explosive blast wave, blunt-force trauma, acceleration and deceleration, or responses to our environment. The initial trauma can result in what's known as diffuse axonal injury or DAI. An explosive blast wave propagated from an explosion causes the brain to bounce back and forth within its casing, the skull. This acceleration/deceleration can cause DAI or the shearing of, or microtears to, the axon. Axons are a component of the nerve cells that allow neurons to send messages between them. DIA disrupts this function with catastrophic consequences.

The same microtearing affects the glial cells as well. This is significant because when these microtears occur, it releases various chemicals in the brain that were only intended to be transported from one location to another location via the vessel. The vessel in this case is made up of the glial cells and the neurons. Think of the glial cells and neurons as an oil tanker. The oil tanker is transporting the message (crude oil) contained in its vessel from one location to another. In the case of the central nervous system, the message is in our neurochemistry, referred to as a neurotransmitter, which is a chemical message transported by the vessel or neuron. When trauma occurs (phase I) and damages the brain (DIA), it can cause the message to be spewed into the brain, just like an oil tanker that has incurred structural damage and is now spewing crude oil into the ocean.

Remember the Exxon Valdez oil spill and the amount of damage it caused the environment when its vessel was damaged, releasing toxins into the ocean? The effects were catastrophic. The damage to our vessels (the glial cells and neurons) causes the equivalent of an oil spill in our brain. This is the process of neuroinflammation of the brain, or phase II. The leakage causes the nerve cells to die and the brain to swell. Here is the kicker: This can happen in a day, a week, a month, or years after the initial injury. How? By the leak from the vessel being miniscule. This builds up over time, eventually killing the surrounding cells and further inflaming the area. This post-traumatic neuroinflammation also leads to the dysregulation of hormones produced in the central gland (neurosteroids) and hormones produced by the peripheral gland (neuroactive steroids).

This silent and invisible injury can go unnoticed for years, making it difficult for physicians to properly diagnose. Patients go to their physician years after receiving the initial trauma to the head or body, having no idea it has affected their health. The patient voices a new complaint with symptoms that were previously not there. Because the right questions are not asked, the underlying condition is not addressed, and no connection is made that these new symptoms could have stemmed from a physical trauma that occurred years ago. The vicious cycle of symptom management is now the focal point.

LESSONS LEARNED

Traumatic Brain Injury is a two-phase injury. Phase I is the initial trauma, referred to as diffuse axonal injury or (DAI). Phase II is the post-traumatic neuroinflammation caused from the trauma in phase I. Post traumatic neuroinflammation also leads to the dysregulation of hormones produced in the central gland (neurosteroids) and the peripheral gland (neuroactive steroids). This silent and invisible injury can go unnoticed for years, making it difficult for physicians to properly diagnose.

The Gordon Protocol: The A=C Scenario

The Gordon Protocol is as simple as it is brilliant. Dr. Mark L. Gordon's groundbreaking presentation at the RAAD Festival (Revolution Against Aging and Death) revealed the **A=C Scenario.** https://youtu.be/DCeUC479Jks

In the **A=B Scenario, Head Trauma (A) = Hormonal Deficiency (B).**

In the **B=C Scenario, Hormonal Deficiency (B) = Psychiatric Disorder (C).**

If **A=B** and **B=C,** then **A=C.**

Dr. Gordon states that we have ignored the hormonal influence over neurobehavior and cognition, or **B=C.** The question is, if you fix **(B)** with replacement hormones in conjunction with reducing neuroinflammation (a.k.a. "The Gordon Protocol"), will **(C)** improve? The overwhelming empirical evidence—based on over thirteen hundred documented Millennium Health Center TBI cases, of which more than 150 have been supported through the Warrior Angels Foundation—is an overwhelmingly consistent *yes!*

LESSONS LEARNED

In the **A=B Scenario, Head Trauma (A) = Hormonal Deficiency (B).**

In the **B=C Scenario, Hormonal Deficiency (B) = Psychiatric Disorder (C).**

If **A=B** and **B=C,** then **A=C.**

Question: If you fix **(B)** with replacement hormones in conjunction with reducing neuroinflammation (a.k.a. "The Gordon Protocol"), will **(C)** improve?

Answer: Yes!

CHAPTER 10

Life Lessons Learned

Standard of Performance: Lessons Learned

DECIDE DEFINE DETERMINE DEDICATE

1. **DECIDE** to live a life worth living.

LESSON LEARNED: Decide to live a life worth living by committing to take action. If you don't like something, fix it. Refuse to give external objects and obstacles power over you. We decide how to receive, process, and respond to the external circumstances of life. **The first step to**

shape one's circumstances is taken in the mind of the Warrior Angel.

PRACTICAL APPLICATION:

I was at my son's hospital bedside when I made the decision to 1) regain my health, 2) return to the man who wrote my Standard of Performance, and 3) find a way to serve others in need. Nothing happened until I made the decision to commit. Deciding to live a life worth living put me on the course to understand and fulfill my purpose. Thinking, visualizing, and believing it first in my mind brought it into existence.

2.   **DEFINE** your life's purpose: the "why."

LESSON LEARNED: "Why," in the context of this book, refers to the reasons for which we exist, our individual purpose. It is attained by an internal charge to seek out answers to the problems of one's life and to fulfill those tasks. The journey to why is a solo mission; it must be undertaken and fulfilled alone. The mind, regardless of its programming, drives our physiology and well-being. A positive mind drives purpose, and purpose is the driver of fulfillment. Placing others' needs ahead of our own drives the kind of purpose and fulfillment one can only begin to imagine. **Serving something bigger than one's self is the *why* of the Warrior Angel**

PRACTICAL APPLICATION:

I falsely believed my life's purpose was being fulfilled as a Special Forces operator. Being an athlete, first, and then an operator didn't fulfill me. They were the temporary vehicles that fueled my fulfillment. The suffering I endured was ultimately self-chosen. I became consumed with myself, by what I thought were unfair circumstances. I lost the ability to remain an operator, I felt I was being mistreated, and I thought I would never be able to regain any purpose or find any significance to my life. I didn't understand there were abundant options for fulfillment.

Choosing to master my thoughts allowed me to focus on the tasks at hand: to heal myself for the benefit of both my family and me, and then to help others heal. That decision allowed for a clear understanding of my "why," to live a life of fulfillment, no matter where I was able to find it. Living a life of fulfillment was, is, and will always be the driving factor of my life. Poet Robert Byrne said, "The purpose of life is a life of purpose." If you're not sure of your purpose, invest your time, thoughts, and energy in helping others.

3. **DETERMINE** how, using the three P's: plan, prepare, and perform.

LESSON LEARNED: Understanding the why permits the creation of the how. Establishing how to plan, prepare, and perform enables us to measure the effectiveness of an outcome against the why. If a particular circumstance, thought, belief, or individual doesn't bring us closer to the why, we're at fault. It's our responsibility to ensure our thoughts, behaviors, and communications work in a manner that brings us closer to our why, not further from it. Immediately identify and let go of the circumstances, thoughts, beliefs, and individuals that don't support your why; give them no dominion over you. Create relationships in which both of you encourage, sharpen, and help the other to realize each other's own unique purpose. **The internal drive and resolve to dare and do what one must, and what others won't, produces the *how* of the Warrior Angel.**

Plan: Build a detailed strategy for seeking out answers. Design a blueprint to fulfill those tasks.

Prepare: Identify, secure, and make ready the tools required to execute.

Perform: Execute to the best of your ability.

PRACTICAL APPLICATION:

If your why is big enough, the how will be illuminated. Deciding to live a life worth living—by defining my why—enabled me to determine how to achieve it. My plan was to get better. The same actions (over and over) produce the same results, and I have no time for actions that don't produce results. So I sought out alternatives. I prepared myself mentally to only strive for behaviors and relationships that would enable me to accomplish the task at hand. This made the Purple Heart, trauma insurance, and Social Security Disability denials irrelevant. This made the financial hardships of a medical retirement and Chapter 7 bankruptcy worth it. Those circumstances afforded me opportunities to seek and find new answers. If a door was closed, I kicked it open. If I had to travel and take vacation time to get treatment, that's what I did. If one treatment modality didn't work, I looked for another.

My command refused to reimburse Becky's travel to visit me while I was at Walter Reed after promising they would, required me to use vacation time to seek outside treatment, questioned my ethics, and conducted an Army Regulation 15-6 investigation to determine misconduct on my part, all to no avail. I didn't let any of that stop me. It would have been easy to just give up, but I knew in my heart that I was doing the right thing. Having a plan allowed me to envision what the end should look like. This gave me the ability to prepare my mind and all of the additional tools I needed. Thinking, visualizing, and believing the plan in my mind allowed for the successful termination of dependency upon dip (chewing tobacco), alcohol, and all medications. It also allowed me to find the protocol that identified and treated the underlying condition for my injury, bringing about the return of the man identified in my Standard of Performance. Laying the foundation, designing the plan, and preparing how to execute it allowed me to perform when the situation called for it. Every decision I made was easy because I had established the tools for dealing with it. I would only engage in thoughts, actions, and relationships that brought me closer to my purpose. I immediately let go of anything I found to be otherwise.

4. **DEDICATE** yourself to others with selfless acts and service.

LESSON LEARNED: Self-actualization begins when our conscious and subconscious minds come together to fulfill a purpose that is greater than ourself. Synchronizing both hemispheres of the brain empowers us to create the life we desire and the world in which we aspire to live. Living a self-actualized life of dedication is the key to unlocking a higher consciousness and a greater love. The dedication to serve something bigger than oneself brings on a level of purpose and fulfillment that is difficult to describe through the spectrum of human experience, but it is attainable. **Shaping circumstances in both triumph and disaster is an art and a science mastered by the self-actualized Warrior Angel.**

PRACTICAL APPLICATION:

Changing my mind-set fueled my commitment to live a life worth living. Defining my "why" allowed me to better understand the driving forces of life: contribution, purpose, and fulfillment. The path to "how" was illuminated by the immutable determination to commit and define my life's purpose. Taking the focus off of myself and dedicating it to my family and to serving others in need ended a life of suffering and delivered a life of abundance.

CHAPTER 11

Final Thoughts

I have since added "My Ideal Self" in support of my SoP. Every morning I sit and meditate on becoming that man with the agreement that I won't get up until I have become my ideal self.

My Ideal Self

I am certain, I live in a peak state of purpose and fulfillment realized in the love and gratitude found in contributing and performing to the best of my abilities in the service of others. Every thought, emotion, action, and means of communication serves to elevate myself and everyone I come in contact with. I earn it every day. Of this, I am certain!

Placing others' needs ahead of our own with consistent acts of selflessness provides for the kind of meaning and success we can only begin to imagine. Once I shifted focus to the beautiful things in life, my life instantly became beautiful. There was no time for an existence fueled by fear, stress, hate, anger, and worry.

To paraphrase popular thinking, energy flows where the mind goes; like attracts like. Choosing to live a life of appreciation, love, contribution, purpose, and fulfillment opened me up to receive the greatest truth. Thinking, visualizing, and believing according to these principles uncovers a personal power that can only be described as Heaven on Earth. When things become hopeless— or even when life is good—find a way to make what you do about somebody else.

SUPPORT WARRIOR ANGELS FOUNDATION

Warrior Angels Foundation (WAF) is a 501(c)(3) non-profit organization founded by Adam and Andrew Marr. A portion of every book sold will be donated by the authors to WAF.

Please visit our website (www.waftbi.org) for more information. Please share this book and the mission of WAF with your family and friends.

WAF MISSION:

Warrior Angels Foundation provides a personalized assessment and treatment protocol, which pinpoints - and, more importantly, treats - the underlying condition for U.S. Military Service Members and Veterans who have sustained a Traumatic Brain Injury (TBI) while in the line of duty.

ABOUT THE AUTHOR

Andrew Marr is the Co-Founder and CEO of Warrior Angels Foundation, is on the leadership team of The Magic Flow Bus, and host's the Warrior Angel Podcast. Andrew is married to Becky, the love of his life, and together they have six children.

The Warrior Angel Podcast

Andrew Marr, a retired Special Forces Green Beret's lessons to his children. Lesson's paid for in blood. Listen at (www.waftbi.org)

The Magic Flow Bus

Perform better. Feel better. Flow better. Access high performance flow states on demand through experiential learning. Level up your life with experts in medicine, art, technology and ancient practices. Become part of the next renaissance of human evolution at MagicFlowBus.com

Morgan James
Speakers Group